"As Mrs. Miller tells her story to the world, sharing her pain, empty resolves and then ultimate victory in the tragedy of child abuse, she ministers to a need Christians seldom admit."

Charisma

"Kathy Miller should be commended for laying bare her personal struggle..... Anyone who battles uncontrolled emotions will find this book helpful."

Today's Christian Woman

"This impressive publication, mingled with tears and smiles, reveals God's guidance—even available for you today!"

Baptist Standard

"As we go with her through her struggles, we are encouraged to know that we aren't alone with these emotions, and that there is hope."

Christian Bookseller

"It must have taken a lot out of this unusually brave young woman to share her story, but there is no telling how many people will be helped by it."

The California Southern Baptist

"I can identify with your situation in many ways.... After buying your book, I read it in two sittings. I couldn't believe how much I could feel your feelings as you wrote each paragraph. How the tears rolled down my face as I read on. As I finished the last chapters, I used my red pen so I could underline important advice. I want to thank you for being obedient to the Lord. Your book has helped me."

A Reader

D1279558

Help For Hurting Moms ...
And Hurting Kids, Too!

Kathy Collard Miller

Foreword by Luci Swindoll

Evergreen Communications, Inc.
Ventura, California

HELP FOR HURTING MOMS....
AND HURTING KIDS, TOO!

Published by
Evergreen Communications, Inc.
2085-A Sperry Avenue
Ventura, CA 93003
(805) 650-9248

Cover Art by Dianne Beck.

Library of Congress Cataloging-in-Publication Data

Miller, Kathy C. (Kathy Collard), 1949–
  [Out of control]
  Help for hurting moms ... and hurting kids, too! / by Kathy Collard Miller.
    p. cm
  Previously published as: Out of control.
  ISBN 0-926284-02-9 (trade pbk.) : $8.95
  1. Miller, Kathy C. (Kathy Collard), 1949–   . 2. Christian biography—United States. 3. Child rearing—Religious aspects—Christianity. 4. Child abuse—Case studies. I. Title.
BR1725.M447A3   1990
248.8'431'092—dc20
[B]   90-3810
                                                CIP

99 98 97 96 95 94 93 92 91 90 9 8 7 6 5 4 3 2 1

Printed in the United States of America

Help For Hurting Moms...And Hurting Kids, Too! was previously published under the title *Out Of Control*.

Dedicated to
Larry
my husband, lover, and best friend

Acknowledgments

I want to thank Virginia Muir, whose encouragement at my first writers' conference gave me the original impetus to begin writing a book about child abuse. A year after that, Fritz Ridenour suggested I write my story and this book was begun. Thank you, too, Fritz!

I also want to acknowledge my friend and neighbor, Patricia LaGraffe, who faithfully prayed for me through each chapter.

To my publisher, Mary Beckwith, I owe much gratitude for her desire to make this book live again.

Most of all, my loving gratitude goes to my husband, Larry, who supported me as I wrote and who encouraged me to share our victorious story.

And to my wonderful children, Darcy and Mark: You are God's gifts to me. I love you.

And my thank yous go to the readers of this book under its original title, *Out of Control*, who confirmed in their letters to me that God has, indeed, used it in their lives.

Contents

Foreword
11

A Word From Our Author
13

1

I Just Want to Be a Good Mom
15

2

But You Promised You'd Babysit the Kids!
19

3

Whatever Happened to the Joys of Motherhood?
23

4

Where Did My Clean House Go?
27

5

Lord, Help My Unbelief
33

6

A Soap Opera and a Bag of M & Ms®
39

7

A Glimmer of Hope
45

8

Punishment Is Retribution, But Discipline Is Training
49

9

At Times It's Difficult, But I'm Learning to Say No
57

10

Lord, Why Won't You Change My Husband?
61

11

What A Relief to Have Others Know
67

12

I'll Show Them My Love!
75

13

The Party Was a Success, But the Price Was High
81

14

Love Is a Choice, Not a Feeling
87

15

It's a Growth Process—For My Child *and* Me
93

16

Success Happens One Day at a Time
99

17

God Loves Me and So Do I!
105

18

On My Way to Victory
111

19

A New Love for My Child
119

20

Christmas—A Day for Starting Over
123

Epilogue
129

Appendix I

How to Deal with Anger
When Stress Becomes Distress
How to Cope with Worry
131

Appendix II

Helpful Resources for Moms
139

Questions for
Individual or Group Study
145

Foreword

This is a courageous book, written by a brave woman. I say brave because it takes the quality of mind and vulnerability of spirit to expose openly one's areas of weakness for all the world to read, especially when that deficiency has been a source of personal embarrassment and condemnation. Some will say that writing a book about such weaknesses is a pronounced act of betrayal against one's own self-worth. However, I don't look at it that way.

To me, while Kathy Miller's writing reflects her disproportionate sense of perfectionism with resultant bouts of anger and guilt, that is not the most important message of the book. The message that is written between the lines is of even greater value: Any person who finds him- or herself in the human condition—and that's every one of us—is enslaved to a nature and its corresponding emotions which can run wild, take over, or be the guiding force in one's life, until those emotions are recognized, admitted, and confessed to God for His regeneration and correction. Everybody has some hidden "something" which is impossible to disregard or to curb, apart from the strength and hope that Jesus Christ provides as we learn to rely upon Him and His Holy Spirit.

Kathy Miller had the courage to reach out for that hope, and it worked! God met her where she was, and He continues to meet her as the need arises, because He is true to His promises and she is willing to believe what He has said. She has my greatest admiration as a fellow struggler.

Luci Swindoll

A Word From Our Author

Parenthood. Motherhood. Fatherhood. Oh, what beautiful sounding words those are to an expecting couple. But rarely do they stop to wonder whether or not they have been trained to be good parents. It's not until the dirty diapers, teething cries, and sleepless nights come that the new father or mother cries out, "Where are all the joys of parenthood I heard about?"

I went into motherhood with joy and excitement like many before me. I had heard very little about the negative side of mothering young children. I know now that when I became a mother I had a very naive and idealistic view of parenting. But reality wasn't far behind. And I didn't cope very well with reality. Instead, I reacted with anger, hate, and violence.

I share my story with you, dear reader, in an honest, vulnerable attempt to clear away some of the myths about parental anger and child abuse. My prayer is that this book will provide hope as well as tangible help for those who are struggling with anger and the frustrations of parenthood. I also pray that this book will help motivate others who at times find themselves out of control to seek the help and support they need. Finally, I hope it will encourage any person to believe that God can help them in their problem, whatever it may be.

Kathy Collard Miller

1

I Just Want to Be a Good Mom

March 1

Two-year-old, blonde-headed Darcy splashed in the bathtub amid suds and toys.

"Time to wash your hair," I announced.

"No, no, Mommy. No wash hair. Please."

"Oh, yes. It's all sticky. It'll feel good to get it nice and clean," I coaxed.

Darcy broke into tears as I rubbed the shampoo into her hair. Suddenly she began rubbing her eyes and yelling, "It's in my eyes. It hurts! It hurts!"

"Oh, it is not," I responded. "There are no suds near your eyes. Besides, it's baby shampoo—it doesn't sting."

She screamed louder.

Without warning, I was engulfed with exhaustion. The pressures that had been mounting throughout the day overwhelmed me and I felt weak. The room seemed to close in on me. The dampness and heat made my clothes stick to my skin. Pushing limp hair away from my forehead and gritting my teeth, I hissed back, "Darcy, there's no shampoo in your eyes. Now hold still or you're in big trouble! Hold still, I said!"

Shrieking, my little girl clawed at her eyes. I turned on the faucet and jerked her to it, pushing her whole head under the running water. Soap flowed down over her face into the tub. She sputtered and coughed, but I didn't care. She was going to get clean whether she liked it or not.

I hurriedly turned off the water. Grabbing her arm, I yanked her out of the tub. Darcy stood shivering and crying. I screamed at her again and again. "The next time you'll hold still when I tell you. We'll do it the way I say and that's that."

I felt like an erupting volcano of hate. Anger and frustration boiled inside me like hot lava. At that moment I felt like I wanted to kill her.

Spanking her with my hand, I found an outlet for my tension and exhaustion. But spanking became uncontrolled beating, until Darcy's hysterical shrieking brought me back to reason. I carried her into her room and dropped her into bed. Slamming the door behind me, I bolted down the hall sobbing.

"Oh, Lord Jesus," I gasped. "I hurt Darcy again. I keep saying I won't do it anymore, but I can't control my anger. What's wrong with me?"

I knelt beside my bed and cried for a long time. Darcy's muffled cries reached me, suffocating me in a blanket of guilt.

My thoughts hurled through my mind like hailstones in a storm. *I've been a Christian for ten years; how can I be so angry? I lead a Bible study and other people think I'm a strong Christian; how can I be acting like this?*

I wanted to scream, "Help me! Help me!" but I was ashamed and frightened. *What if they take my kids away from me? What if everyone knows I abuse my child?*

I'm not a child abuser! I defended myself. *Or am I?*

"I'm still hurting her," I cried out. "I'm abusing my own child. Oh, God, no!"

The word *abusing* echoed through my mind like a boulder thudding down a canyon wall—strong and final.

There was no hope. I had prayed; I had cried; I had begged for deliverance. *If only Larry didn't have to work at night, he could relieve some of the pressure. How long can I continue like this without seriously injuring Darcy or baby Mark?* Darcy's frightened face flashed before me, wrenching my heart like a tree being uprooted by the wind. *I don't want to hurt them. I love them. I want to be the best mother in the world. But I'm so far from that.*

"Oh, Father," I whimpered. "Help me! You've got to. I can't help myself!"

I turned my attention to Darcy and couldn't hear her crying anymore. Walking quietly to her room, I opened the door and peeked in. Her naked body was huddled by the pillow. She saw me and started crying again. Pushing aside my shame, I pulled her pajamas out of her drawer and started to dress her. Her body grew tense at my touch.

"Don't be afraid, Darcy," I said. "I'm not mad at you anymore. Mommy was wrong to hurt you. I'm sorry. I wish I could promise you I'll never get angry with you again—but I can't. Oh, how I wish I could." My tears plopped onto the sheets beside her. I gently tucked her into bed and left the room.

As I put on my nightgown, I wondered if God cared, or if He had deserted me. *Of course not, Kathy,* I chided myself. *You know better than that. God is always there.*

Then where is the help I need? I wanted to shout. But I pushed the doubt out of my mind as I cried myself to sleep.

2

But You Promised You'd Babysit the Kids!

March 10

Ignoring Thursday and Friday as they passed, I clung to one anchoring thought of sanity: Saturday would be here soon. Larry had agreed to take care of Darcy and Mark so I could go clothes shopping. The thought of being out in the real world—all by myself for the first time since Mark was born three months ago—excited me.

Saturday morning finally arrived. As I survived Darcy's temper tantrum at the breakfast table and Mark's dirty diaper, I looked forward to those few hours of peace and quiet while browsing in the mall. Even though several stubborn pounds refused to yield after my pregnancy, I wanted to find a new outfit to enhance my appearance—and boost my spirits.

By the time Larry sleepily walked into the kitchen around ten o'clock, I had verified the checkbook's presence in my purse two different times.

"Good morning, sweetheart," I joyfully greeted him. "You look rested. Your breakfast is on the table and the kids are clean and happy. I'm hoping I'll be back by lunchtime."

Larry's baffled look set off warning bells in my mind.

"Where are you going?"

"Don't you remember? You said I could go clothes shopping today."

"Oh," he muttered. "I forgot. In fact, I don't really remember saying that at all."

"But, honey, you said on Monday that Saturday would be a good day for you to take care of the kids."

He still looked bewildered. "I'm sorry, Kathy, but I told Ken we would fly to San Diego today. He's wanted me to take him for a long time, and today's the only day he can go. And that Cessna® I've been wanting to try out is available at the flying club. I guess you'll just have to go another time."

My throat tensed with disappointment. Despairing thoughts jumbled my words. "But, Larry, you promised. I've been waiting all week for today. I've just got to get out for a while. You don't know what it's like..."

"Well, I'm really sorry, but I promised Ken. You can go shopping any time."

Any time. Oh, sure, any time, except when you're flying or when you're working your "part-time" second job in real estate or when you need to sleep ten hours a day. Right, any time.

Angry tears clouded my vision as I furiously wiped the counter. I knew from experience that, no matter how long I might continue to debate, the case was closed.

Thirty minutes later when Larry kissed Darcy good-bye, the tenseness in my throat crept into my neck. He shut the back door behind him and my rage surfaced in sobs and cursing. I choked on the apple I was eating and was so infuriated that I hurled it at the door, splattering it over the walls and ceiling.

"Larry," I shouted, "I hate you. I hate you. Can't you see our relationship is dying? Sometimes I wish you wouldn't come back. Your plane can crash for all I care."

Frantically, I stumbled to my bed, knelt on the floor, and cried out my anguish to God. I imagined the scene of Larry's funeral. Friends and relatives told me how brave I was to be so strong. They didn't know that I was delighted in his death. I was free.

"Mommy, Mommy, cartoons are over." Darcy's announcement snapped me out of my self-indulgent reverie, and I slowly pushed myself up knowing Larry's dirty breakfast dishes and Mark's hungry cry awaited me.

When Larry returned that evening, Darcy's excited greeting drowned my silence.

After tucking the children into bed, I told Larry good night.

"How come you're going to bed so early?"

"I don't feel well. It was a rough day." I hoped he wouldn't press me further. I didn't even want to talk with him.

"All right. I hope you feel better tomorrow. Good night."

Lying motionless in bed as tears trickled down my cheeks and onto my pillow, I wanted to scream my pain at him. *If you really love me, spend more time with me. Choose me instead of your other activities.*

Then I rebuked myself. *That sounds so selfish. I can't say that.*

But the feeling that I wasn't first in his life continued to chip away at the foundation of our marriage.

Later, when he quietly pulled the covers back and gently slipped into bed, I pretended to be asleep. However, it wasn't until I heard his steady, deep breathing that I finally relaxed and truly fell asleep.

For the next couple of days I struggled to blow out the flame of my anger and bitterness. But like a trick birthday candle, it rekindled each time I thought about Larry's insensitivity toward my needs. I felt depressed and helpless, as if I were riding a raft down a coursing river, without oars or a rope. And my distress calls to God seemed to be unheard.

On Tuesday afternoon after Larry left for work, I loaded the children into the car and we left to visit my friend Jill. She greeted me at her door, casually dressed in worn jeans and a green turtleneck sweater. Her red-haired, eighteen-month-old son, Aaron, toddled after her.

We settled comfortably on her newly upholstered plaid couch to watch the news on TV and chat. Aaron and Darcy sat on the floor and scribbled with their crayons as Mark lay on my lap chewing on a rattle.

After a while, the newscaster related a story about a couple who had been arrested for child abuse. My heart started beating hard and I took a deep breath.

"You know, Jill, sometimes I understand how parents might be tempted to mistreat their children. Kids sure can make parents angry." Laughing nervously, I looked at her and hesitantly waited for her reaction.

"Well, I sure can't," she retorted, shaking her head. "Those people are awful. They ought to be arrested."

I jerked my head away, hot tears stinging my eyes. *Lord, am I really that bad? Doesn't anyone else get angry like I do?*

Gratefully, I heard Jill's phone ring. While she was gone, I wiped away my tears and vowed never to let anyone know how angry I could become. Later when I drove home, I concluded that, in some way, I must not be allowing God to help me. And in an attempt to change, I affirmed my commitment out loud, "Lord, I promise to pray more every day." Yet, I knew my vows had been ineffective in the past. A seed of doubt sprouted within me.

3

Whatever Happened to the Joys of Motherhood?

March 20

Darcy's training pants were wet again! Again! I couldn't believe it. She had messed them only forty-five minutes ago. She had promised she would tell me the next time she needed to use the bathroom.

Marching over to her, I directed her into the bathroom. I struggled to pull down the soaking pants. *What am I doing wrong? I'm afraid she's never going to learn.*

"Darcy, you're supposed to come into the bathroom and use the potty chair. Remember you promised Mommy you would go in the potty chair. Why can't you learn?"

She's doing it on purpose; I just know it. We've been going through this for several months now. She's done it right before, so I know she can do it. She just refuses to obey me.

"You went potty in your pants. I'll just have to spank you."

"No, no, Mommy. I won't do it again." Her pleading seemed to confirm my speculation.

"From now on you'll go in the potty chair, do you hear?" Hitting her wet bottom and gritting my teeth, I grumbled, "I am sick and tired of wet pants...dirty pants...puddles on the carpet...loads of extra laundry...getting up in the middle of the night to change your soaking sheets."

My tortured thoughts ricocheted in my mind. *You're so much trouble. I can't do anything or go anyplace when I want. You demand love that I don't have. I don't want to be a mother!*

My hands grabbed for her throat. As if I were watching a scene from a murder movie, I saw myself choking my child. Seconds later, her horrified face and fear-paralyzed body somehow satisfied me and I jerked my hands away. But I was terrified when I saw red marks on her neck. Suddenly, Darcy began screaming hysterically.

I ran out of the bathroom. Making my way out the door to the back patio, I pounded my fists into my thighs and cursed myself. "What have I done? I've been doing so well. Oh, God, please help me. I'm out of control again."

Maybe I should call someone for help. If I called my pastor, I wonder what his reaction would be. I've never had any kind of therapy before. What would people think of me? How could I tell the ladies in my Bible study that I was going for counseling? They might not respect me any more. They might think God doesn't have the answers. After all, if He hasn't helped me, they'll think He can't help them.

No, I'm just going to have to deal with this myself. I know God can help me. I just haven't found the exact answers yet, but I know I'll do better. Maybe if I increase my devotional time and read more Christian books, it will help.

I could hear Darcy crying in the bathroom. *Oh, thank you, Jesus, that Larry is gone. He just doesn't under-stand how I can get so angry. I try to tell him, but he can't believe it. I suppose I should be grateful that he doesn't feel anger like I do, but if he did, at least he could sympathize with my feelings.*

Taking a deep breath, I walked back to the bathroom. When Darcy saw me, she backed up to the wall. "It's okay, Darcy. I'm not mad anymore," I tried to reassure her. But when she didn't relax, my heart only felt heavier. I dried off Darcy and then put another pair of training pants on her. The red marks on her neck were slowly fading.

"Darcy, please remember. The next time you have to go potty, come into the bathroom and use the potty chair. Mommy has a piece of candy for you if you go potty in the potty chair. Mommy doesn't want to get angry with you, but I really think you're ready to be a big girl and wear big girl panties. Then you won't have to wear baby diapers. You can be a big girl with panties like Mommy wears."

Darcy's tear-stained face looked up at me, attempting to smile. "Okay, Mommy, I try."

The next day before Larry left for a business appointment, I asked, "Do you think Darcy's ready to be potty trained?"

"Well, I don't know. How has she been doing?"

"Not very well. At times she manages just fine, but then she'll go for a long time without success. Sometimes I wonder if she wets her pants on purpose."

Larry laughed. "You sound like you think she hates you and wants to get even."

All of a sudden his comment didn't sound so far-fetched. "I wonder if she does."

"Oh, come on, Kathy. She's just a little girl."

"No, really. Sometimes when she disobeys me, I think she's doing it on purpose to show me I'm not a good mother. And when she has her temper tantrums, I think I'm a bad mother because I can't make her happy."

"I didn't think you were supposed to make her happy, just obedient."

"But what about the joys of motherhood I always hear about? I'm not a very joyful mother these days."

"Well, I know it's not easy to be a mother, but I don't think you're supposed to be joyful all the time. You're not perfect and neither are the children, you know."

"I guess I'm not. I just want to be."

Larry looked wrapped up in thought.

"What are you thinking?" I asked.

He stared at me and said, "I wonder if you want Darcy to be potty trained as early as possible so that your success can be a credit to your mothering?"

At first I started to tell him that his comment was ridiculous, then I caught myself. "I really hadn't thought of it that way before. I know I don't want to continually change diapers. But maybe I also want her to be a billboard for my mothering accomplishments. She's almost two-and-a-half. I thought for sure she would be trained by now. But maybe she isn't ready. I think I'll give her a few more days and see what happens."

The next few days were disastrous. Instead of getting better, she had more accidents. I wondered if my violent outburst had set her back.

All right, Lord, I think you're showing me she's not ready, so I'll put her back in diapers. I guess it's better than washing a load of training pants every day.

Darcy didn't object to being put back in diapers. I was surprised. In fact, she immediately seemed happier and more obedient. *Well*, I thought, *maybe I did the right thing for once in my motherhood career.*

4

Where Did My Clean House Go?

April 1

Mommy, Mommy, wake up. I hungry."
Roused from my peaceful dream world, I wanted to shut out Darcy's insistent plea. *Oh, no, not so soon. I was awake nursing Mark only minutes ago. How many times did he wake up last night...three...four?* My fogged mind had lost count. I focused my eyes on the digital clock next to the bed and moaned as I read 5:49.

"Darcy, you can play in your room for awhile. I'm too tired to get up right now. Let Mommy sleep a little longer."

"No. No. I hungry. Come, Mommy, come." She tugged at the sheets.

Larry murmured in his sleep beside me. I knew that no amount of pleading could convince Darcy to leave me alone. Her talking would only wake Larry and he didn't get to sleep until three-thirty in the morning because he had worked overtime.

"Okay, just a second. Let me put on my slippers." Only determination pulled my body out of the warm bed as exhaustion adhesively clung to my muscles.

I stumbled into the kitchen. Dirty dinner dishes lay scattered on the counter, painfully reminding me that I had decided not to wash them the night before. Why had I thought it would be easier to do them this morning? And then I remembered. I had taken the time to vacuum the carpet instead, because it was littered with Darcy's cracker crumbs. I felt better. At least one thing was clean.

I piled greasy dishes into the sink and started cooking oatmeal. I smiled as I remembered that my family's reunion was being held in the mountains tomorrow. Thoughts of sitting outside the cabin in the cool, fresh air, visiting with my family and relatives inspired me to work even faster. Then, out of the corner of my eye, I noticed Darcy running through the family room. Her foot caught on the plant stand, sending the philodendron to the floor. Darcy lay sprawled and crying on the floor amid soil, bits of leaves, and broken pottery.

"My clean carpet! Darcy, look what you've done." Again, anger erupted within me like hot lava.

Gritting my teeth, I grasped Darcy's arms and yanked her to her feet. I felt uptight, ready to explode.

Darcy's chin quivered as she attempted to control her sobs. "Hurt, Mommy. Owee."

A voice within me said, *It was an accident. She's so little.* Suddenly, my heart softened. Unexpectedly, I remembered the last thought I had before I drifted off to sleep the night before: *Lord, I commit tomorrow to you and whatever you might have in store for me.*

"It's all right, Darcy. I know it was an accident," I said, while brushing the dirt off her pajamas.

I looked down at the broken pieces of blue pottery littering the floor and started crying. "That's the planter my neighbors gave me when my daddy died. I hope I can glue it back together," I sobbed. "Lord, it's just not fair. Not only does it seem like I can't go anywhere, I can't even spend my time in a clean house. Why did I have kids, anyway?"

Vacuuming up the soil, I couldn't control the tears that dribbled down my face. *I am so sick and tired of never having this house clean. There is always something that needs to be done. Before Darcy was born I only needed to spend two or three hours a week cleaning and everything would stay nice for days. Now I spend every day cleaning one mess after another and picking up countless toys along the way. Any time I dream of setting aside for myself is consumed by endless loads of laundry and stacks of dirty dishes. I can't put my favorite knickknacks on the coffee table, and now even my favorite planter is broken!* My self-pitying monologue continued in my mind until the dirt was gone and breakfast was served.

Later that morning, Darcy started sneezing and soon I was wiping her runny nose. By evening, her stuffy nose and hacking cough confirmed my fears: She had a cold.

"Wouldn't you know it! Wouldn't you just know it!" I complained to Larry. "We're supposed to leave for the mountains tomorrow and Darcy gets sick. Why can't the Lord have a little mercy on me? I want to go to the reunion so desperately. If Darcy doesn't get any worse I'm going anyway, no matter what. I just don't care. My fun isn't going to be spoiled by a sick kid."

But Larry's frown made me realize I couldn't risk either Darcy's health or contaminating everyone else.

Through the night I repeatedly attended to Darcy's needs. She coughed and coughed and medicine didn't seem to help. By the time the morning sun arose I had wearily accepted the fact that Darcy was worse and had resigned myself to staying at home.

Why is God doing this to me? Is it because of the way I've been treating Darcy lately? Is He trying to punish me? I know I deserve to be punished, but I have always believed that my Lord is loving and forgiving. He knows I don't hurt her on purpose, yet why can't I break my anger habit? I've seen Him work positively in other areas of my life. Why is this problem so different?

As the day progressed, I unsuccessfully attempted to believe God loved me. Physical exhaustion sapped my emotional strength. I was constantly yelling at Darcy. It seemed she couldn't do anything right. And when Larry awoke, I nagged at him too. He had left the house earlier than usual, saying that he needed to work on a flight plan.

After Darcy and Mark went down for their naps at one o'clock, I gasped at the disarray of the house and began to straighten up the mess. But eventually I became so weary that I lay down on my bed, convinced I would rest for just a few moments before cleaning up some more.

Abruptly, I awoke and glanced at the clock: 3:05. *I can't believe it. Darcy doesn't usually sleep this long. She's not even coughing. Wow, I feel pretty good. But the house...Now, I've wasted all that time.*

I threaded my way through the house, picking up toys, books, and newspapers. Just removing the clutter made each room look better. At least I had accomplished something.

I guess a nap is a good idea. I'll have to take more of them. "Thank you, Lord, the house looks better."

But my pleased feelings soon surrendered to self-pity as I thought about the fun everyone—except me—was having at the reunion. Through dinner and into the evening, my warring thoughts battled for control of my mind.

The Lord gave me a good afternoon. I got to rest and still picked up the house.

Yeah, but why couldn't I go to the mountains? God could have protected Darcy from getting sick, a part of me said.

He must have wanted me to stay home for some reason, came another voice.

Yeah, but I could have been a witness for him to my family... On and on the battle raged.

The next few days I noticed that when a joyful attitude temporarily won a skirmish, I abounded in energy. But when boredom and selfishness reigned, my energy level decreased, and depression waved a victory flag.

Several days later as I listened to a Christian radio station, a pastor shared a message about the importance of memorizing God's Word. Of course I had done that in the past, but now I wondered if this could be a part of the solution I needed. My devotions that day covered Psalm 42, and when I read verse 11, I rejoiced. "Why are you in despair, O my soul? And why have you become disturbed within me? Hope in God, for I shall yet praise him, The help of my countenance, and my God."

That's it! I'll memorize this verse and every time I start to feel discouraged or tired I'll say it.

Now my inward dialogue turned into praise. Each time a debilitating thought entered my mind, I repeated the verse. Soon, all I had to tell myself was "hope," and a smile would come to my face. In addition, I took a nap every day. Physically and spiritually stronger, now I was able to handle Darcy's sickly disposition during the day and frequent night feedings with Mark.

My spirit sang. I was on the way to victory. After all, hadn't I passed the test of coping with Darcy's sickness and my exhaustion? It had been more than a week since I had been out of control. I knew I would never hurt Darcy again.

5

Lord, Help My Unbelief

April 15

L arry, Mark has been sneezing all day. Do you think he's coming down with Darcy's cold?"

"Well, I suppose he could be."

"You know what that means, don't you? We might not be able to go to your parents' house for Easter. We're supposed to leave next week."

"Oh, that's right. And since I'm flying us in the Cessna®, we won't have an air-pressurized cabin. That could hurt his ears if he's congested."

Fearful thoughts swirled around in my head. I felt like kicking trust and faith out the door in locked suitcases. *What if we can't go? I'm so looking forward to getting away to Larry's parents' home in the high desert. Even though it's a little more difficult to take care of the kids there, it's nice to visit with Larry's folks and not be responsible for meals and cleaning. I really need to relax there. Larry and I could play tennis at the local high school or take walks in the clear, crisp, evening desert air.*

"Oh, please, Lord, heal Mark of his cold. I've been good with Darcy and promise to continue. And, remember, I didn't get to go to the reunion. So could you please make Mark better by next week?" I bargained.

Four-month-old Mark continued to sneeze, and the next day it was difficult for him to nurse because he couldn't breathe through his stuffy nose. Gently stroking his short blonde hair away from his warm forehead, I appealed to

God: "Father, I'm believing that you'll make Mark better soon."

But if I believe, then why do these nagging doubts harass me like a pesky fly incessantly circling my head?

"Lord, I'm trying to believe. Help my unbelief."

The next morning, I opened my eyes slowly, surprised that the sun was already up and the house was still quiet. Hadn't Darcy woken up yet? I guessed not. For just a few moments I relaxed as the sunshine ignored the drapes and craftily invaded the room. Larry slept peacefully beside me. I climbed out of bed, went to the window, and turned on the air conditioner's fan. Its steady, dull buzzing would help drown out the morning commotion.

Walking through the quietness, I breathed a sigh of gratefulness. "Thank you, Father. Mark's congestion hasn't prevented him from sleeping."

But then my apprehension of the previous day resurfaced. *What if Mark isn't even well enough for us to drive there?*

I began to fix oatmeal, knowing Darcy would wake up soon, and tried to shove my distrust to a corner of my mind, like a child attempting to push down the puppet in a jack-in-the-box.

Only a few minutes later, I heard her bedroom door open. She walked sleepily into the kitchen, rubbing her eyes, her faded pink blanket trapped under one arm.

"Hi, sweetheart. Did you sleep well?"

"Mommy, what we do today?"

"It's Monday, so we're going to Bible study. You get to play with the children at Julie's house."

"Goody, goody," she exclaimed as she broke into a little skip.

Hearing that recently learned phrase made me giggle. Darcy looked so cute as her little round face lit up with excitement. She could be so darling. The ambivalence of my feelings pierced my heart as I realized how much I loved her when she was good and how much I hated her when she disobeyed. But my thoughts were interrupted as the telephone rang. It was Esther, our regular babysitter for the Bible study children. She was sick and wouldn't be able to babysit this morning. I thanked her for calling and hung up. *Oh, no, who am I going to get this late? Sometimes I wish I weren't in charge of this Bible study.*

I quickly finished preparing breakfast. *Please, Lord, help me find someone else. I don't want to have to stay with the kids. You know how much I look forward to that Bible study and the Wednesday morning La Leche League meeting. They are my only opportunities to get out of the house. Please!*

The fear of not finding a babysitter for Bible study and of not being able to go to my in-laws haunted the recesses of my mind, as I quickly fed Darcy and dressed Mark. Darcy jabbered her usual one hundred words per minute, but I didn't seem to hear as I mentally made a list of sitters to call.

"Mommy! Mommy! I want to paint!" Darcy's repetitious whine finally permeated my brooding.

"No, Darcy, you can't paint this morning. We don't have time. I still have to get ready for Bible study and find a babysitter."

"Mommy! I want to paint!" Darcy's insistence grated on my nerves as if someone were scratching their fingernails on a blackboard.

"Darcy!" I shouted, "I said no. Now stop your whining!" My jumbled thoughts tumbled over themselves. *Mark's not getting better. I've got to get a babysitter. I don't want to stay with the children!*

Suddenly, Darcy's face turned red. She started screaming and jumping up and down in rage. I grabbed her arm, whirled her around, and hit her bottom hard...four, then five times. "You stop that right now!" I heard a crack from her shoulder as I yanked her into the air by one arm. Yet, I remained angry while I carried her, feet dangling in the air, into her bedroom and pushed her onto the floor. "Now stay there until you can be quiet."

After slamming the bedroom door, I stood trembling in the hall. I listened carefully, fearfully expecting Larry to emerge from our bedroom. But I only heard the humming of the fan, Darcy's crying, and the exaggerated pounding of my heart.

I walked to the phone, muttering, "I've got enough to think about without putting up with her nonsense."

I started calling my list of babysitters, but when I had exhausted it without luck, tears blurred my vision. *I don't want to spend two-and-a-half hours with those children. I can't even handle my own. It's almost nine o'clock...only thirty more minutes. I guess I don't have any choice now.*

I dressed quickly and ran a comb through my hair. Then I called Sally, who taught the study, to let her know I would be taking care of the kids.

"Kathy, just a minute. My mother is here visiting. I'll ask her to take care of them. She loves children."

"Do you think she would?" The hope in my voice made me feel guilty, so I quickly added, "No, I couldn't ask her to do that. It wouldn't be fair."

"Oh, it's okay. Hold on; let me go ask her."

My heart beat hard. *Oh, Lord, please make her want to do it. Please!*

Sally came back on the phone. "Kathy, she says she'll be glad to. Really, she loves to do things like this. I'll be teaching, so she doesn't have anything to do anyway."

I couldn't hide my enthusiasm. "Oh, that's great. I'm so glad. I'll meet you at Julie's house."

Thank you, Lord, you did it. I still can't believe it. Thank you, thank you.

I rushed to Darcy's room. Surrounded by her dolls and toys, she looked at me in surprise. "We go now, Mommy?" she asked.

"Yes, honey, we're going. I'm sorry I got angry with you earlier. But we have to hurry now." I knelt beside her, pressing gently on her shoulder. "Does your shoulder hurt?"

"No."

I couldn't feel anything wrong, so I quickly dressed her.

A few minutes later at Bible study, as the six of us sat around Sally's dining room table studying in the book of Ephesians, I continued to thank the Lord that I was there. When it was time for prayer requests, I asked that they pray for Mark to recover quickly from his cold. As one of the ladies in the group prayed for him, I felt hopeful. Yet doubt still lurked in the back of my mind.

The next day Mark seemed worse and my faith plummeted like a glider caught in a downdraft.

That week I struggled to build a wall of faith, but I continually allowed examples of God's seemingly negative responses to my prayers interfere with my construction. Then I recalled how God had supplied a babysitter for the children at Bible study on the previous Monday morning, and another small wall was erected. Back and forth, the bricks were piled high and then knocked down again. Forgetting to use the mortar of Scripture promises, I appeared to be a clumsy stonemason.

On Friday, Mark seemed slightly better. He took a long nap and nursed better than he had all week. My hopes soared. I planned what I would pack for the trip to Larry's parents' house.

Saturday morning arrived, and the moment of decision faced us. Larry and I talked it over and finally decided that the remaining congestion was not serious enough to cause Mark's ears to hurt while in the plane.

As we flew out of the airport Sunday morning, I cautiously nursed Mark to keep him sucking so his ears would stay clear. During the flight, I reflected on the past week and berated myself for my fluctuating faith. *Lord, all my worrying didn't do a single bit of good. Why couldn't I have just trusted you all along? It was your grace in answer to all the prayers that made Mark better for this trip. Worrying only made me tense and unhappy and didn't change a thing. I blew it again, didn't I? I lost control with Darcy. When am I ever going to master my anger?*

I looked at Darcy in the backseat. She was asleep. The softened features of her face made her look angelic and peaceful.

Darcy, I'm sorry. I'm trying. I'm really trying. I couldn't stand it if I ever injured you. I'd kill myself.

Tears flowed down my face. I looked out the side window so Larry wouldn't see my grief. The houses and cars below looked small and unimportant. *Lord, is my anger ever going to be an insignificant part of my life? Will I ever be able to look back and see myself in control?*

I was afraid to think any further. *I must live one day at a time. Today is Easter Sunday, celebration of the day Jesus rose from the dead. I'm going to believe I have resurrected control over my anger and my doubts, starting with this trip. Thank you, Father, that we can go. I know it's a gift from you.*

6

A Soap Opera and a Bag of M & M's®

April 30

As I finished dusting the living room furniture, I turned to Larry and said, "Honey, have you noticed the bills that have stacked up since we got home from visiting your parents? When do you think you'll be able to send them off?" I tried not to sound as uptight as I felt.

"Oh, I guess I can do them before I go to work. But I want to finish this article first."

For a moment, I studied Larry relaxing in the blue, corduroy lounge chair and reading the magazine that seemed to represent the barrier between us. I pleaded, "Honey, it wouldn't take you more than fifteen minutes to write out those checks. Could you take care of it now, please?"

Glancing up at me, he tartly replied, "Kathy, don't worry about it. I'll do it later."

Don't worry about it? Doesn't he know how much I hate to see bills accumulate? But I caught myself. *I'm not going to nag him. I must trust the Lord. It's not my responsibility anymore. I turned financial matters over to Larry. Now he'll have to deal with the consequences if the bills aren't paid.* Then the thought of paying late charges, when we barely had enough money to cover the bills, began to gnaw at my determination to trust God. I remembered how I used to agonize over paying the bills on time and how I begged Larry to take over the job. When he had finally said he would, I was glad and so relieved. But now I wondered if I had done the right thing.

Father, I don't want to nag him, but you aren't motivating him. Don't you think as Christians we should pay our bills on time? Please tell him to take care of them!

As that Monday afternoon passed, I realized it would soon be time for Larry to leave for work and he still hadn't made any move toward the desk. I tried to keep busy putting the kids down for their naps and cleaning up the lunch dishes, but my mind lingered on the overdue bills.

After he had left for work and I knew he hadn't touched the checkbook, I fled to the family room. "I'm going to scream, God. I can't handle it. If I write out those bills myself, I'll be doing them for the rest of our marriage. I'm not going to do it. He'll just have to pay the consequences."

I frantically eyed the room. *What can I do to take my mind off this?* I rushed over to the television and jerked it on. I flipped the selector around several times and finally found a soap opera I hadn't watched for several months. I tried to reassure myself. "Now, I'm not going to get hooked again. I'll only watch it today. I've got to do something to get my mind off those unpaid bills."

Within the first fifteen minutes, I had become reacquainted with the plot. Then the first commercial came on advertising a new cake mix. I nestled among the pillows on the couch, enjoying the picture of the richly frosted devil's food cake.

"That sure makes my mouth water!" I tried to think of any sweets around the house that might satisfy my craving. I smiled as I remembered the large package of M & M's® I had bought. Rustling through the cupboard, I found it and returned to my chair just in time to find out that Sue was on trial for murdering her husband even though Kevin had really shot him.

By the end of the program, I had finished half the bag of candy. Scouting the kitchen, I finally decided to hide them in the potato bin.

The next morning Candace phoned. She wanted me to help her organize and teach a ladies' Bible study in her neighborhood.

"Wow, Candy, that's great," I exclaimed. "What a wonderful opportunity. How many are interested in coming?"

She explained her plan for the study and then mentioned, "We're going to have it in the afternoon. That's the best time for the ladies to meet."

"Oh..." I quietly replied, my shoulders drooping with disappointment.

"What's wrong, Kathy?"

"That just wouldn't work out for me. My kids take their naps then, and there's no way they can miss them. I guess I won't be able to help you."

After I hung up, the sadness in my heart overwhelmed me. "Lord, I want to serve you so badly. I long to reach out and minister to others. Why won't you let me? Why am I stuck home with these children?"

Looking over at Darcy as she watched "Sesame Street," I could barely keep from darting glances of hate at her. I knew God wanted me to be a loving mother and raise godly children, but somehow it just didn't satisfy me. I remembered the excitement of starting my own neighborhood Bible study many years earlier. So many neat things had happened as a result of that study. I wanted to reach out to others again.

Lord, I want to be used by you like that again. Didn't I write down as one of my goals for this year, "Start another Bible study"? Instead of evangelizing the world, all I do is pick up toys, change diapers, and wipe runny noses!

For the rest of that day, I thought about the candy waiting in the potato bin and tried to determine whether or not Pamela would tell Mark that she was pregnant by Louis.

At three o'clock, I grabbed the M & M's® bag and flipped on the television. A load of guilt lay heavy on my heart, but I rationalized, "Well, I don't have anything exciting to do around here, so I might as well see what's happening with them."

The next two weeks were consumed with more and more TV- watching and candy-eating. The candy filled me up and eventually I only nibbled at dinnertime. I was engrossed with the soap opera characters and their problems. At times they seemed more real and important than my own family.

By Friday, my patience level had crumbled. I took the children for our usual early evening walk. When Darcy wouldn't stay out of the street, I grabbed her shoulders and shook her violently. Embarrassed by my behavior, I yanked her into one arm, pushed Mark in his stroller with the other, and practically ran home.

"Darcy, we won't go for any more walks if you can't obey me. One of these days you'll learn to mind me." Feeling my face flush, I slammed the front door behind us.

Darcy screamed, "Walk. Walk. I want a walk."

Suddenly, I realized how tired I was. My muscles felt as if they were attached to one-hundred-pound weights. I gazed at the family room. Coloring books, crayons, and bits of crackers littered the floor. I wondered how long it had been since I had dusted the furniture. I couldn't remember.

Now, Kathy, you really are tired—just hang on, I tried to encourage myself. *Don't let Darcy get to you. In just a few hours both children will be asleep and you will be able to go to bed too.* The thought of the cozy, warm bed made me feel even more exhausted.

The evening dragged. Darcy continued to be keyed up and unhappy. Mark cried for seemingly no reason. I decided he must be teething.

Finally, after putting them to bed, I put on my pajamas and slipped between the sheets of my own bed. *Oh, this feels so good. I'm so tired. I hope I'm not getting sick.*

"Father," I began my bedtime prayer, "why does it seem like I never get anything done around here? My house is always a mess, I don't think I'm a very good mother, and I'm too weary to be a good wife. Am I really worth anything? How can you love me?"

My tired body and heavy heart sucked me into a pit of hopelessness. It seemed as if I would never learn the lesson God was trying to teach me. The days merely passed by uneventfully—except for the anger that wrapped a strangling cord around my existence.

Maybe I just need a good night's sleep. Help me tomorrow, Father... But before the thought was finished, I had drifted into a restless sleep.

7

A Glimmer of Hope

May 10

Mark's hungry cries startled me out of a deep sleep. The sun's rays barely permeated the overcast sky; the high clouds made it seem more like a June morning than one in the middle of May. Dragging myself out of bed, I wondered why I was still so weary. Even after ten hours of sleep, my body felt as though I had just run a marathon.

Plodding through the morning routine, I suspected I was coming down with a cold, but I didn't feel congested. I comforted myself with the promise of a nap.

Mark went down for his nap easily, but Darcy wouldn't settle down. As I lay down on my bed and started to relax, Darcy wandered into my room, her thin, blonde hair damply matted against her head.

"Darcy, you're supposed to be in bed sleeping. Now, go back to your room."

"Mommy, me not tired. Can I color, please?" Her bright, alert eyes convinced me she really wasn't sleepy.

"Oh, all right. You can color here on the floor while I rest." A warning bell in my brain signaled potential danger, but I assured myself that I would keep an eye on her while I rested.

I got up, found the crayons and coloring book, and spread them out on the carpet beside my bed. Then I strictly cautioned her, "Now remember, Darcy, you color only on the paper and nothing else, okay?"

Her happy face anticipated coloring in her new Lassie coloring book. I smiled, lay back down on the bed, and watched her scribble on the first page.

Oh, this feels so good. My muscles relaxed, and as I closed my eyes, I felt peaceful, more peaceful than I had felt in the last couple of weeks. *This feels too good to be true...*

Suddenly, I sat up straight. I was still in a daze when I realized that I had drifted off to sleep and had completely lost track of time—and Darcy. She was gone. I looked around the room. Half the crayons were scattered about the floor, and the closet door featured quite an assortment of red crayon circles.

"Darcy! Darcy! Where are you?" I implored.

Oh, no! All the walls will be crayoned. As I felt a burning flash of anger sear through my body, I wondered whether I was more angry with Darcy or myself.

I ran down the hall, following the crayon-marked walls. Turning the corner to her room, I stared in disbelief as Darcy sat on her bed drawing on the wallpaper.

"Darcy! Look what you've done. You brat, look what you've done!" *How am I ever going to get all these marks off so that Larry won't know what happened?*

I grabbed Darcy by the shoulders and lifted her into the air. Face to face, I screamed, "Darcy, I told you not to color on the walls. Why won't you behave? Can't you do anything right?"

I shook her. Her head wobbled back and forth as she looked at me in wide-eyed horror. "Brat, brat, brat! Sometimes I hate you."

In my mind's eye, I imagined hurling her onto the floor, her body landing with a dull thud. *I'm going to do it; I want to hurt her,* something in me said.

A second later, the reality of my thoughts gripped me. I sat her on the bed. "Oh, God," I sobbed. "I really could have hurt her. I don't hate her. I hate myself. What am I going to do?"

I threw my arms around Darcy's trembling, whimpering body and hugged her tight. "I'm sorry. I'm sorry. It was my fault you colored on the walls." I coaxed her onto my lap and gently rocked her back and forth.

"Why am I so irritable and angry, Darcy? I just don't understand it."

As Darcy cried softly, I surveyed all the bad times we had had during the last couple of weeks, and one common denominator stood out: the candy! Our worst days were ones when I had eaten lots of sweets. All that candy was making me tired and irritable. My body was reacting to the sugar. In addition, I hadn't been eating nutritious meals.

"Father, thank you. Thank you for showing me. All right, I won't have anymore candy. I promise."

But that afternoon as three o'clock loomed closer, I was haunted by the two candy bars that were hidden in a seldom-used pan in the cupboard. I bargained, "Well, I'll just watch my soap opera and not have any candy. How's that, Lord?"

Before I could hear His answer, I turned on the TV and immediately became engrossed.

As I sat leaning toward the television, I glanced into the living room where Darcy played near a five-gallon bottle of drinking water the delivery man had left earlier that morning. *I wonder if she could break that bottle? No, I don't think so; it's awfully heavy. How could she possibly push over such a . . .* But before I finished wondering about the possibility, Darcy pushed on the bottle. With a soft crunching sound, the bottle fell over and broke, spilling five gallons of water onto the green, sculptured carpet. Shocked by the accident, Darcy jumped back, then stared at me in fear.

An overwhelming sensation of surrender flowed through my body as I helplessly watched the water soak into the carpet.

"Yes, I see it, Darcy. It's okay, honey. I'm not going to get angry with you. Mommy wasn't taking good care of you. I finally see how wrong I am."

I turned off the television and began picking up the hundreds of pieces of glass.

"Father, you sure got my attention. I confess that I've been neglecting my family and I've been eating a lot of junk. I ask you to forgive me."

During the next hour, as I used almost every towel in the house to soak up the water, a thought that had been rambling through my mind for the last couple of months resurfaced. *I wonder if my children will grow up and say, "My mother didn't have time for me."*

Lord, I don't want my children to say that. I really want them to feel as if I'm always available and that they are very important to me. I know I complain a lot about being a mother, but actually I want to be a good mother. I don't know why I have such a hard time enjoying what I really want to be. Why do I, Lord?

Even though no voice answered, I felt peaceful. Sugar and incessant television-watching were no longer going to dominate me and make me irritable. I was determined to spend my time and energy focusing on the Lord. I knew it was going to be different from now on.

Darcy intently watched me spread towels and walk on them to help soak up the water. "Darcy, I promise you that I'm going to try to spend more time playing with you. Would you like that?"

She ran into her room and returned carrying her Candyland® game. "Can we play now, Mommy?" she pleaded.

I laughed, enjoying her enthusiasm and sparkle. "Oh, my daughter, Darcy, you are a live one. As soon as I finish this, we will play Candyland®!"

8

Punishment Is Retribution, But Discipline Is Training

May 20

D arcy, I really need to clean the bathroom right now. Mommy is having a Tupperware® party tonight, and I have to clean the house. I know I promised last week to play with you more often but today I must concentrate on the house."

Darcy's pout wrenched my heart. Even though I had meant what I had said the previous week, each day's busy schedule had pushed aside my good intentions.

"Okay, how about after I finish the bathroom? I'll stop for a few minutes and we'll play one game of Candyland.®"

"Okay, Mommy. I get it ready." Her disappointed pout instantly turned into a radiantly happy smile as she skipped off to her room.

By the time I put out fresh towels, I realized how fast the morning was vanishing. I knew I should bake the cake so it would have time to cool before I frosted it. I wondered if I could start it before playing with Darcy.

Candyland® is such a simple game. Why do I dread playing it? I knew why. It seemed like every time we almost reached the winning candy house and the end of the game, one of us would draw the lollipop card or the gumdrop card and be sent back almost to the beginning. Sometimes the game would continue for hours. And the fact that Darcy inevitably folded the cards or threw them around the room added to the irritation. I would be glad when she was older and we could play more sophisticated games. But I reminded myself that if I didn't want to play with her now, she probably wouldn't want to play with me then. I feared the consequences of not spending enough time with Darcy in these early years and felt guilty about my selfishness. *Oh, Father, will I ever be the mother I want to be?*

"Well, enough of this," I scolded myself. "I've got to get busy."

I tiptoed into Darcy's bedroom and peeked around the corner. She was carefully laying out the colored cards around the Candyland® board.

Oh, good, I thought. *She's busy, so I'll go start the cake.*

But I had not even finished combining the ingredients when Darcy ran into the kitchen carrying a handful of Candyland® cards. "Mommy, ready to play?" she asked.

"Oh, honey, I'm sorry. I decided to mix this cake first. Can you wait a few more minutes, then we'll play?" I tried to sound cheerful, hoping to ward off a temper tantrum. At first, as her lower lip started to quiver, it seemed that I was going to be unsuccessful. But then the phone rang and distracted her.

"Me get it, me get it," she yelled.

"No, Darcy, only Mommy and Daddy answer the phone."

I watched Darcy out of the corner of my eye as she walked away folding two cards in half. Oh, well, at least she didn't have a fit.

I picked up the receiver and sadly listened as a friend told me she wouldn't be able to come to the Tupperware® party. I felt disappointed but tried to sound understanding as I accepted her apology.

Turning my attention back to the cake, I realized I couldn't hear Darcy. I walked into the living room to check on her and stopped short. She was sitting on the fireplace hearth, sprinkled from head to toe with sand from the gas logs. A thicker layer of the sand encircled her on the bricks and carpet.

"Darcy!" I screamed. "What are you doing? I've told you over and over again to stay out of the fireplace. Just look what you've done. I'm trying to keep everything clean for company tonight."

I marched over to her and yanked her to her feet. "Why can't you do anything right?" I hollered as I spanked her. And, even though my hand stung, I continued to hit her again and again.

Darcy's screaming egged me on. "Maybe if it hurts enough, you'll obey me next time."

When I could no longer stand the pain in my hand, I pushed Darcy down on the couch. Ignoring her sobs, I jerked the vacuum out of the hall closet, snapped it on, and furiously pushed it back and forth over the sand. Occasionally, I glared at her and lectured, "Why do you continue to do the things that you know make me so mad? I can't understand it."

Darcy's tear-filled eyes pleaded with me. When my anger subsided and all the sand had been vacuumed up, I sat down beside her. "Darcy, Mommy has told you before that you are not to play in the fireplace. I just don't understand why you keep doing it. I don't want to get angry with you, but I'm so uptight about getting everything ready. Please help Mommy by doing what I tell you, all right?"

Darcy rubbed her eyes. I knew I should give her some attention, but the thought of not being ready for the party made my neck muscles tighten. I rationalized, "I'll get everything ready for tonight, then I'll have time to play with you."

For the rest of the day, I cleaned the house, prepared the refreshments, and kept a close eye on Darcy. Mark woke up early from his nap, fussy from teething, and needing to be held, so I didn't get everything done as quickly as I'd hoped. It was five o'clock when I finally finished. With a sigh of relief, I plopped Darcy on the floor in front of the television to watch "Sesame Street" and then fixed dinner.

When only eight people arrived for the Tupperware® party, I realized that there had been no reason to get uptight or angry and regretted that I had spent so much time cleaning the house, instead of playing with Darcy.

During the following week, Darcy's behavior continued to deteriorate. Every time I started a cleaning project or sat down to nurse Mark, she found a way to get into trouble. She emptied soil out of the houseplant pots even though I repeatedly spanked her. Her jealousy toward Mark increased; when she thought I wasn't watching, she pinched him or hit him. Her disobedience was getting worse, but it seemed as though I was powerless to stop it. Spankings didn't deter her. I thought she would want to avoid my anger, but instead the struggle for power was intensified— and so was my guilt.

I was convinced my anger was at the root of Darcy's temper tantrums. I kept thinking that if I wouldn't get so angry with her, she wouldn't disobey. The more I thought about it, the more I realized that I was trying to be perfect. For some reason, I believed that if I were perfect, Darcy would be too. *That's ridiculous*, I chided myself. *You'll never be perfect and neither will Darcy.* I knew then that I should work on getting my anger under control, and that I shouldn't expect Darcy to always obey me. After all, what child always obeys his parents? Somehow, that realization relieved my mind.

However, I did think I should give Darcy more attention. At times, I knew that I was neglecting to fill her emotional needs. *Why does cleaning the house seem more important than paying attention to Darcy?* As I looked around the house, I realized that a neat house gave me tangible proof that I had accomplished something. When I gave Darcy attention, I didn't have any concrete evidence that I had done anything worthwhile. She still disobeyed me! Plus, it was difficult to give Darcy the love and attention she needed because I didn't feel very loved myself.

I longed for the days before Darcy was born, when Larry and I did so much together. Larry had been the companion and best friend I'd always wanted. But now that our lives were so busy, we were growing farther apart, and my nagging pleas for Larry's attention only widened the gap between us.

Just as I begged for Larry's attention, Darcy's disobedience pleaded with me, "I need you. I want your attention and approval."

But I could think only of my needs and would respond harshly: "Then why don't you obey me and be a good girl?"

Little did I know that her answer would have been: "Because, then, you won't pay attention to me at all."

Several weeks later at Bible study, one of the women raved about a book she had just finished reading entitled *Help! I'm a Parent* by Dr. Bruce Narramore.[1] I asked her if I could borrow it sometime and she excitedly brought it over that afternoon. By the time I was halfway through it, I could understand how I was failing by punishing Darcy rather than disciplining her.

In the book, Dr. Narramore explained the difference between punishment and discipline. He said that punishment is retribution, but discipline is training. The focus of punishment is on the past misdeed, whereas discipline focuses on future correct deeds. When he suggested positive use of the phrase, "Mommy will have to spank you so that you will remember not to do that again," I memorized it and practiced saying it over and over again.

As I continued reading, I recognized that I had been inconsistent in my spanking. Sometimes I would spank her for something she did wrong, but other times I would let the misbehavior slide by. For the first time I also realized that my anger was not going to create an obedient spirit within her.

I was excited! I could hardly wait for Darcy to misbehave so that I could try the new disciplinary techniques I had learned. I didn't have long to wait.

The next morning I discovered Darcy playing with the telephone. Just two days before, I had spanked her for doing the very same thing and here she was doing it again. Anger started to well up inside me, but I seized control and decided that this was the perfect opportunity to try out my new method of discipline. I took a deep breath, walked over to her, and said, "Darcy, you know that you are not supposed to play with the telephone." Then, I almost said, "I'm going to spank you because you played with the telephone," but I remembered the phrase I had memorized and instead stated, "Darcy, I am going to have to spank you so that you'll remember not to play with the telephone the next time."

I guided her to her bedroom and told her to stay there. I went to the kitchen and took the wooden spoon out of the drawer. As I walked from the kitchen back to the bedroom, I reminded myself I was training Darcy, not taking revenge for her disobedience. I was surprised at how calm I remained.

When I returned to Darcy's room, she mischievously grinned at me, probably reasoning that she wasn't in trouble because I wasn't angry. Picking her up and holding her close, I explained again, "Mommy is spanking you because I love you and because I want you to remember not to play with the telephone." I gave her three quick swats across the bottom. She started crying as if she were going to have a temper tantrum, but I continued to hold her close. She stopped crying within two minutes. Blinking back tears, she penitently murmured, "No more telephone, Mommy."

I wanted to jump for joy. I rejoiced, "Oh, thank you, Jesus; this is the way it's supposed to be. I didn't get angry. I didn't spank her too hard."

For the next couple of days, I calmly used the spoon each time Darcy disobeyed. Soon, all I had to do was tell Darcy I was going to get the spoon and she would immediately obey.

I was ecstatic. It seemed too good to be true. I was seeing

effective results from disciplining Darcy correctly. I congratulated myself, "I'm actually doing something right."

Note:
1. Dr. Bruce Narramore, *Help! I'm a Parent* (Grand Rapids, MI: Zondervan, 1979).

9

At Times It's Difficult, But I'm Learning to Say No

May 30

"Hi, is Kathy Miller home, please?"

I shifted the telephone receiver to the other ear. "Yes, this is she."

"Hi, Kathy. I'm Ruth from the church office. We're calling to see if you'd consider teaching one of the pre-school Sunday School classes this summer. Our summer session starts in two weeks, on June thirteenth, and lasts until school starts. We'd really love to have you help us."

Hesitating, I grappled for words. "Well, uh...oh, I see. Well...I have taught a children's Sunday School class before, but that was a long time ago."

"I can understand your concern, but our teaching materials are excellent, and, of course, you'd have an assistant to help you."

My thoughts tumbled over each other. *I wonder whether she would be so quick to ask me if she knew I abuse my child. Considering I can barely cope with my own kids, I wonder how I'd handle the pressure of teaching. But they always need people to help. I really should do my part.*

The pause became awkward. I strained to say something. "Well, I'd like to help because I really appreciate everything my daughter learns in Sunday School. Uh, I guess there's no reason why I can't...but I really should talk it over with my husband. How about if I call you back tomorrow?"

"That would be fine. I'll look forward to hearing from you then. Good-bye."

"Good-bye."

I hung up and anxiously faced the reality of knowing what Larry would say. He usually contended that I had too much to do already and should drop some of my activities. I would defend my position and say that I needed opportunities to get out of the house. Certainly, I wasn't looking forward to talking with him about this situation.

As I thought more about teaching the class, I began to wrestle with my feelings of "duty." *Shouldn't you do your part? If Darcy's receiving, you should be giving. If you don't do it, who will?*

Visualizing Darcy's faithful teacher and her happy welcoming smile each Sunday, I wondered if I could find joy in taking care of other children when I didn't even enjoy my own.

The next morning after Larry woke up, I explained, "Larry, one of the ladies from church called yesterday and asked me to teach a children's Sunday School class for the summer months. You know, Darcy learns so much at church, and I want to do my part. What do you think about it? I bet I could handle it. I'm sure it wouldn't take very much time." I hesitantly smiled at him, trying to appear convinced myself.

His eyebrows frowned over his hazel eyes. "Well, I'm not sure you have the time to do it. And even if the preparation time were short, you'd still have the pressure of getting it done. Right now you barely have enough time to keep the house clean."

I could feel a mass of hurt begin to grow within me. "But, Larry, I really feel obligated to help. What if no one helped? Darcy wouldn't be learning more about Jesus."

Larry's grin assured me that he knew I wasn't really convinced myself. "Honey," he pleaded, "you just don't have enough time or energy. You are so busy with Mark because he's still just a baby. And Darcy is a handful. I'm proud of you for wanting to help, but you'll just have to trust the Lord to supply someone else to fill the gap. He can do it, you know."

When Larry rose from his chair, I knew the discussion was over. I reluctantly admitted to myself that what he said was true, but guilt overwhelmed me anyway. *Why do I have such a hard time saying no to anyone? That must be the hardest thing for me to do. I've accepted more commitments than I can handle just because I couldn't refuse someone's request.*

For most of that day, I tried to get up the nerve to call Ruth back. Over and over, I rehearsed my lame-sounding excuses. By the end of the day, I still hadn't called. Every time the phone rang, I jumped, fearing it might be Ruth.

Shortly after dinner, I discovered Darcy playing with the telephone for the second time that day. "Darcy, I told you earlier you can't play with the telephone. Why do you keep doing it?"

Then it hit me. I had been so uptight about calling Ruth that I hadn't been disciplining Darcy. I'd been giving her all sorts of yelled warnings but had taken no action.

I smiled at her. "Well, little girl, I guess it's time to get back on course again."

The next morning I forced myself to dial the church's number. When Ruth answered, I explained that my husband didn't think I had enough time to fulfill such a responsibility. I falteringly went on to explain that our son was still a baby and required a lot of attention. As I went on and on with all my excuses, I knew I was verbalizing insecurity.

Ruth politely accepted my explanations and said she was sure the Lord would provide someone to teach. I hoped so, but wondered how he could if people like me didn't do their part.

Feeling foolish, I hung up. I rebuked myself. *Your imma-*

turity shows when you can't give a simple explanation or say no. What weak faith you have when you can't trust the Lord to fill a need.

Then I remembered something a friend had shared with me several months earlier. She had learned that "a need is not necessarily a call." At the time she had repeated it to me, the phrase hadn't meant much, but now I mulled over its significance. If someone expresses a need to me, it doesn't necessarily mean that God intends for me to accept the challenge.

Even as I sighed in relief, guilt knocked at the back door of my emotions. But I didn't let it in. "No. No! I'm not going to feel guilty again. I've got too much to do now without taking on new responsibilities. For one thing, I've got to work on controlling my anger," I cried out, trying to convince myself.

During the next few days, as I thought about the phrase *a need is not necessarily a call,* I realized that if I accepted a project or a position that God didn't want me to assume, I would be taking away an opportunity from the person whom God truly intended for the responsibility. I would be robbing her of her blessing.

By accepting such a position I might be able to minister to others, but it could also prevent me from being where God really wanted me to be.

This was starting to take shape in my mind: *I don't have to feel guilty. It's up to God to supply for every need, not me. I'm only supposed to do what He wants me to do; therefore I can say no.*

I chuckled to myself as I thought of how often Larry teased me by saying, "Assert yourself!" Now, I knew how I would reply next time: NO!

10

Lord, Why Won't You Change My Husband?

June 8

L arry, have you thought any more about going to the church picnic tomorrow? I really want you to go. It'll be such a great opportunity for us to have a family outing, and Darcy is looking forward to it."

Even as I spoke, my soul beseeched, *Please give him a desire to go, Lord.* When I had first mentioned the occasion earlier in the week, Larry hadn't been sure he'd go. So I had prayed all week that he would change his mind.

Larry turned away. "Well, it looks like I'm going to have a real estate appointment tomorrow."

"If it's in the morning you could come after you finish," I suggested.

Dropping onto our couch, Larry riveted his eyes on me and explained, "Kathy, I don't want to go. I'm sorry, but it just doesn't sound like something I'd enjoy. You go and have a good time with the kids."

A lump grew in my throat and tears darted into my eyes as my spirits plummeted to the ground.

"Honey," I pleaded, "I just don't understand why you don't want to go with us. Please come. Please!"

"Kathy, this isn't the only activity for families, you know. We'll do something together at another time."

I turned and walked out of the room, tears streaming down my face. *Lord, am I so wrong to want us to do*

*things together? Are his real estate deals more impor-
tant than his family?*

I wanted to bang my fists against heaven's gates,
demanding an answer. *Father, why don't you change
Larry? Why don't you make him want to spend more
time with us? I'm so lonely.*

Larry followed me into the bedroom. I brushed away my
tears before he could see them.

"Kathy," he prodded, "are you upset? I promise we'll do
something another time."

I wanted to fling abuse at him, to pour out my hurt and
let it sting him too, but I felt discouraged. What good would
it do? I knew it would only create an unresolved argument.

I began making the bed and in contrived cheerfulness
replied, "As much as I want you to go, I can't force you if you
think you won't have a good time."

"Thank you." His smile deepened my pain.

The rest of the day I stayed away from Larry. A cage of
resentment trapped me inside. Even though I had let
myself in and closed the door with a loud metallic clang,
the sign outside read, "Courtesy of Larry."

The next morning, the thick-barred cage still enclosed
me. But now it was smaller, choking off my ability to
forgive. As I hurried around the house attempting to wash
several loads of dirty clothes and water my houseplants,
Larry wrestled with Darcy on the couch. Her cries of delight
irked me. *He gives Darcy so much attention. Why doesn't
he give some to me? He says he loves me but he won't
even come to the picnic.*

Larry and Darcy's continued roughhousing drove me to
keep busy with preparations for the picnic: making a salad,
forming the hamburger patties, and packing up diapers
and clothes for the children.

When Larry stood, ready to leave, he picked up Darcy,
giving her a big hug and kiss. Standing nearby, I waited for
him to reach over and kiss me. When he walked out the

door with only a "Bye, Kath, see you this afternoon," I silently walked away.

"Darcy, come into your bedroom so we can get ready. We only have a few minutes before we must leave." Noticing the pile of unfolded clothes and the dirty breakfast dishes, I felt the wheels within me turn faster. I rushed about in a futile attempt to slow down time.

"Darcy, I said come into your bedroom," I yelled down the hall. She ran into the bedroom, jerked open a drawer, and flung out an old play suit.

"I want to wear this!" she exclaimed.

I groaned. "But, honey, that's all stained. It's so old, I can't get it clean anymore. Look at this nice new outfit I bought you. It has a cute bear on it."

She shook her head back and forth emphatically. Her thin hair whipped across her face, loosening the barrettes I had put in earlier.

"Darcy, stop moving your head so much, your barrettes are going to come out. Now look, you can't wear that. It looks dirty. Come over here right now and I'll put this on you."

Darcy impetuously threw the clothes down on the floor and jumped up and down, screaming. Her crying grated on my nerves. It seemed as if she were saying, "I have a need and you aren't meeting it. You are a bad mother."

When I couldn't stand it any longer, I barked, "Darcy, stop that right now. I'm telling you that you'll wear this outfit. I'm going to get the spoon. Now stop it!"

Thinking I would move past her to get the spoon, I stood up. Suddenly her rebellious, whining cry overpowered me. "You look like your father and you're just as obnoxious," I screamed at her.

Instead of taking a step, my foot rammed forward, kicking Darcy in the leg. "I can't stand your crying. If you don't stop it right now, I'll kick you again.

Darcy crumpled to the floor, crying out in fear and pain. I

grabbed her shoulders hard, hissing, "I'm sick and tired of your temper tantrums and crying. That's all you ever do." I continued to verbally assault her, letting all my frustration and hate pour out.

In an instant, horror replaced my ebbing anger as I realized what I had done. I burst into tears and knelt beside Darcy as she sobbed. *Oh, God, what in the world have I done? God, God, where are you? Please help me. I've been doing so well, why can't I cope now? When am I going to be able to control myself?*

Larry's gun flashed through my mind. *I might as well die. I'm no good to anyone, especially Darcy. I'm destroying her...and myself.* But I knew that even though misery engulfed me, there had to be an answer other than suicide.

I rubbed Darcy's leg but couldn't feel anything wrong except for a slight bruise. "Darcy, I'm so sorry. I don't know what's wrong with me. I can't seem to help myself. Please don't cry next time. I can't stand it. It tears me apart. I just want to make you happy."

I didn't want to see Darcy's tear-filled face. Avoiding eye contact, I lifted her to her feet and explained, "We've got to hurry now." I dressed her in the new outfit. She didn't complain.

In a blur of agony, trying not to think, I gathered everything together and packed it in the car. Wiping my tear-covered face as we drove down the street, I tried not to look over at Darcy sitting silently in her car seat.

We arrived at the park and I attempted to smile as friends greeted me. Remaining on the verge of tears, I was panicked that someone might comment about my pained look. I spread a blanket for us to sit on and vaguely noticed the clear blue sky and warm, leaf-rustling breeze. My depressed spirits contrasted with the beautiful California summer day. Some families around me relaxed or played softball. Others prepared grills for barbecuing. Darcy excitedly ran to the nearby playground while I settled Mark on the blanket.

I squeezed the last hot tears out of my eyes, embarrassed lest anyone see. Watching the other families happily playing together or visiting with each other drove a knife through my heart. The struggle within me was a waging war. On the one hand, I wanted to accept Larry as he was, but on the other hand, I wanted him to be the husband I needed.

I wanted to scream to heaven. *Why isn't Larry here? Doesn't he love me and his family? Sometimes I hate him. For sure, I hate myself and what I've done. I can't ask your forgiveness, Lord, I'm so ashamed. How can I call myself a Christian? I've hurt Darcy so many times, and I'm afraid I'll do it again.*

Hopelessness consumed my icy heart. The breeze warmed my body but not my soul. Would anyone be sad if I killed myself? I didn't think so—not if they knew the real me, the angry me.

11

What a Relief to Have Others Know

June 10

Saturday and Sunday passed without my acknowledgment. Sinking in a quagmire of depression, I didn't want to face the fact I was regressing. In fear of hurting Darcy again, I tried to avert any conflicts with Darcy or Larry.

At Bible study on Monday, my friend and co-leader, Sally, briefly commented on my gloominess; I told her that I didn't feel well. When she invited me over on Wednesday afternoon to talk about our next set of lessons, I apprehensively wondered if she would try to delve into the reasons for my sullenness. But I assured myself that she sincerely wanted to plan for the next session. How thankful I was that she was helping me guide the Bible study until Mark was older and I could take responsibility for leading it again.

On Wednesday afternoon, with Mark in his stroller and Darcy dressed in shorts on this warm June day, we walked down the block to Sally's house. With each step, more fear swelled within me. *She suspects something's wrong, I know it. But how could she?* The burden I carried was overwhelming. I suspected everyone looked at me with suspicious stares. A part of me dreaded, yet another part hoped for, a confrontation with Sally.

Dressed in jeans and a tailored blue blouse, Sally answered the door in her usual cheerful manner. We settled in her family room and chatted over iced tea. Her bright green eyes sparkled at me, and she smiled with a joy in the Lord that I envied.

I loved to come to Sally's house. I felt peaceful just being there. I could tell she had older children by looking at her immaculate home. Her kitchen counter was clean and neat, and it always looked as if she had just vacuumed her carpet.

"Well, Kathy," she interrupted my thoughts, "have you thought any more about what we might want to study next session? We've got a couple of weeks to order the materials."

We talked about potential topics. Then, after Sally's sons wandered into the room with a balloon, our conversation drifted to our children. Darcy batted the balloon back and forth with them. Perplexed by the strange, yellow floating ball that bounced off his nose, Mark laughed in delight.

"Kathy," Sally commented, "I've never seen Darcy so animated."

"You're kidding," I laughed. "She always has that much enthusiasm, if not more."

"She must be quite a handful. I remember Shawn had that much energy, but Bryan seemed a little calmer. It seems as though God usually gives us children with different personalities. Is Mark calmer or more active than Darcy?"

"Oh, Mark is definitely calmer. He's my little sweetheart. He's so easy to take care of. I sure wish Darcy were more like him. Sometimes I get so upset with Darcy, I could..." I stopped. My palms grew wet and clammy. My mind flashed back to Jill's shocked reaction so many months before.

I can't tell Sally. I'm sure she has never been so angry with her boys that she's wanted to kill them.

My face flushed and I glanced up at Sally. She intently waited for me to finish. "Oh, sometimes Darcy really gets on my nerves," I blurted out.

Sally continued to gaze at me as if I had something more to say. *I wish she wouldn't look at me like that. She won't understand.* But my heart wanted the polluted flood waters that thrust against my emotional dam to be released, so that the reservoir might be refilled with clean, clear spring water. Stinging tears sprang into my eyes. *But if I don't tell someone, I'm going to explode. I don't want to hurt Darcy again.*

"Well," I hesitantly began, "Darcy gets to me sometimes, and I have a hard time controlling my temper. Sometimes I'm afraid I'm going to hurt her. I've taken my anger out on her in some terrible ways."

There, I've said it! The horrible truth is out.

Afraid to confront Sally's condemning look, I glanced the other way. When she started to speak, I cringed inside. *Here it comes. I knew I shouldn't have said anything.*

"Yes, I can remember feeling so angry with Shawn one time that I shook him by the shoulders until his teeth clattered. Those were some very difficult times."

I turned my head toward her, my mouth dropping open. "You're kidding. You did that? I wouldn't have thought you'd do something like that."

Sally laughed. "Oh, sure, I think most mothers feel that kind of rage at one time or another. I certainly hope I'm not the only one."

"But, but...how do you cope? What's your secret?"

"Well, if you mean my formula, I don't have one. Although I have found that when I feel that intense kind of frustration or anger, I try to deal with it in a constructive way."

I sighed with relief. *I'm not the only mother who feels that kind of rage. I'm not alone. Oh, thank you, Jesus. Thank you.*

I wiped the tears from my eyes. *Does she really understand what I've been talking about? Does she realize what I'm telling her? I don't know, but it doesn't matter. She feels strong anger, too!*

"Sally, what are some ways you've found to deal with anger and frustration? I'm really desperate."

Sally's eyes looked distant for a few moments. Finally, she broke the silence and said, "Well, let's see. I think being aware of when I'm under extra stress helps me to control my anger before it starts to control me. My body often tells me through taut muscles or headaches that I'm too tense. I know then I need to make some changes in my circumstances."

"Yes, I can relate to that," I interrupted her. "Now that you've mentioned your reactions, I realize I have a tendency to grit my teeth when I start to get angry."

"Since you recognize that, try to distract yourself from your anger when you begin to grit your teeth."

"What do you mean when you say, 'distract yourself'?"

"Well, you could pound on a pillow, or do some vigorous exercise like running in place, or even play the piano. Just do something to relieve the pressure and give yourself breathing space, so you can think about the real cause of your anger. You see, most of the time when I'm upset with my children, I discover that they aren't the true cause of my anger. It's usually something else that I'm not trusting the Lord for. I really believe that the bottom line of coping with my stress and anger is completely trusting that God is in control of my life—and letting Him have His way."

I knew she was right. I wasn't trusting the Lord for my marriage or submitting to His plan for me as a mother. I always blamed the kids for my anger, but actually I was bitter toward Larry and God for my discontent. I felt hesitant to tell Sally about the unhappiness I felt in my marriage, so instead I asked her, "Sally, will you pray for me about this? I'm really afraid I could hurt Darcy. I've prayed about it for a long time by myself, but I can't seem to get control. Maybe if you pray with me, the Lord will perform a miracle."

Sally nodded. "Of course, I'll pray for you. I'll pray every day that the Lord will reveal what the root of the problem is so that you can dig it out and expose it. And remember, don't be too hard on yourself. God knows you can't be perfect here on earth, so don't expect that of yourself. Only Jesus is perfect. We're still in the process of growing to be more like Him. When you feel really uptight or angry, give me a call and we'll talk about it."

I thanked her. As we talked for a few minutes longer, I felt like bursting with joy. I had revealed my horrible secret and my friend hadn't condemned me or even reacted with shock. She understood! She still respected me as a person and as a Christian. Would her support and prayers be the answer? I hoped so. How I wanted this to be the end of my awful nightmare.

During the next few days and into the weekend, the burden of my anger was gone. I remembered to discipline Darcy consistently, and whenever I sensed I was tired, I took a nap. Sometimes, I called Sally to share my pressures; other times, I jogged in place. More and more often, I could recognize the beginning stages of my anger. My rested, peaceful soul rejoiced in the Lord and I knew Sally's prayers—and mine—were being answered.

During Bible study the following Monday, I sensed the Lord prompting me to ask the other ladies to pray for me and for the solution to my anger. *But, Lord, I don't need any more prayer. Sally is praying for me and I've been doing fantastic. Everything's okay now.*

But the urging continued even though I tried to ignore it. At the end of the Bible study, when Sally asked if there were any prayer requests, I blurted out, "Yes, I have one."

Feeling my face redden, I frantically tried to think of something else for which I could ask prayer. When my mind went blank, I stared at Sally. She smiled reassuringly.

Okay, Lord, if you want me to, I will.

Taking a deep breath, but speaking only slightly above a whisper, I made my request. "Well, I wanted to ask...uh... to ask all of you to pray for me and...uh...my anger toward Darcy. I've been getting awfully angry at her lately and I'm having a hard time coping."

Julie giggled. "Oh, come on, Kathy, you're the last person who needs prayer for that. You're always so calm and cool with Darcy and Mark."

"Yes, Kathy," Mary continued, "I'm sure it can't be that bad. We all get upset with our kids—everybody does. I'm sure you're making a big thing out of nothing."

Frustrated, I looked around trying to formulate my thoughts into words. "No, really, I need your prayers. It's been pretty tough these past few months, and I'm scared. I can't seem to grasp the Lord's power in this area of my life. Darcy gets to me too easily."

By now, everyone's sober face had riveted on me. Julie spoke first. "I'm really sorry I laughed, Kathy. I just didn't take you seriously at first. But I'll remember to pray for you every day. I know the Lord will strengthen you in this area."

"Thank you, Julie. I really appreciate everyone's prayers."

The tension in my chest subsided as the seven women nodded their heads, agreeing to pray for me.

After Sally dismissed us, I felt awkward walking with everyone to the sitter's house. Then Julie spoke up again. "Kathy, I've discovered that if I don't try to repress my anger when I first feel it, I can face it and deal with it better. Repressing it only makes it fester within me."

"Yes, I agree," Mary joined in. "I've also heard that we should communicate our anger through 'I' messages instead of 'you' messages."

"Oh, yeah?" I turned to Mary. "What does that mean?"

"Well, 'I' messages are phrases like, 'I feel angry when that happens.' Whereas, 'you' messages are words that imply blame like, 'You make me angry.' If I explain how I feel instead of blaming the other person, that person is less likely to become defensive about what I'm saying. And I have opened the door for better understanding and acceptance of my anger."

I nodded my head. I didn't completely understand all that she meant, but I was beginning to see that there was a lot I needed to learn.

Then some other members of the Bible study, Pat and Anne, shared times when they had been angry with their children; I could see they were really trying to help. The

Lord did want me to share my experiences. He was going to use everyone's prayers.

When we reached the babysitter's house, I opened the door and saw Darcy playing on the floor with blocks. When she saw me, she raced over to me, hugging my legs. Full of hope, I lifted her into the air and kissed her.

"Darcy," I whispered, "I love you, and from now on things are going to be great."

12

I'll Show Them My Love!

June 20

Honey, this is really a nice restaurant," I commented. "I'm so glad we came here."

"I thought you'd enjoy it. After all, it's not every day we get to celebrate our seventh anniversary. Happy anniversary!" Larry raised his water goblet into the air. I lifted mine to meet his; we gently clinked them together in a toast.

Seven years before, on June 20, 1970, we were married. But at this moment, I could hardly believe it. I scanned the restaurant noticing the antiques and old-fashioned decor, which enhanced the romantic and nostalgic atmosphere. I watched Larry sitting across from me, peacefully enjoying his gourmet dinner of crab. As I savored my prime rib, I mused over the ten years since I had met Larry at a high school water polo game.

"Do you know what the most significant part of our history together is for me?" I reflected out loud. "It's how the Lord used you in my life to bring me to Him. If you hadn't taken me to your church, I might not have heard that Jesus wanted me to know Him personally. Thank you, honey."

Larry's grin caused a flood of emotions to well up within me. It was that same easygoing smile I remembered from our courting days, the smile that had made me feel so special. My insecurity had thirsted for his love and acceptance. Imagine! A guy had actually accepted me just as I was. I began to feel the joy of that stability and love again. Then I remembered it was seven years later, and the familiar, tormenting loneliness of the present brought me back to reality.

If Larry really loves me as he says he does, why doesn't he spend more time with me? Oh, sure, it's easy for him to take me out for our anniversary, but what about the way he treats me on the other days of the year?

The insecurity and loneliness I had experienced before I met Larry returned, and I started to believe that his love and devotion had never been real.

Larry broke into my thoughts. "Sweetie, you look so sad. What are you thinking about?"

Pushing my creamed peas around on my plate, I stammered, "Oh, I was just thinking about...about how you met so many of my needs when we were dating."

"Well, don't I meet them now?" he laughed.

I tried to laugh. "Well, I would love for you to spend more time with me."

Larry's smile faded. "Oh, that again. I've told you I'm trying to gain financial security for our family, and that means I need to work longer hours. Believe me, it'll pay off in the end. You'll see."

My chest tightened in the familiar way that helped me recognize tension and stress these days. "Sweetheart, I know you want to do that. But I would rather have you around than have more money. I want you."

Larry rolled his eyes upward. "You just don't understand. I've explained it to you before."

Oh, no, now we're going to argue on our anniversary night. Boy, did I say the wrong thing. How can I put my feelings into an "I" message? But rather than risking the possibility of saying the wrong thing again, I desperately tried to talk about something else.

"Have you noticed that Mark is sitting up by himself for a few seconds already?" I tried to giggle. "He's such a good baby. I hope he lives through Darcy's picking on him."

Larry's effort to laugh at the changed subject made me

realize the argument had been dropped. We were at a truce again.

For the rest of the evening, we skirted the issue of Larry's long working hours. Instead, we talked about our birthdays, which would be celebrated the following week, and about the family birthday party my mother was planning for next Friday.

It was now Friday afternoon, and I was excited about the party. Evidently, Darcy sensed the excitement too, because she wouldn't stay in bed for her nap.

"Darcy, we're going to be up late tonight at the birthday party. You've got to go take a nap," I explained.

I walked her back to her bedroom. "Mommy, I not tired. I want to play," she whined.

"Now, don't start whining," I commanded her, my voice rising. "Please, Darcy, try to sleep. You'll be happier tonight if you're not tired. Now, just lie there and try."

I walked out of her room sensing that my trust in God's plan was being eroded by worry. *Lord, if she doesn't sleep, she's going to be a brat tonight. I don't want to have to come home early. Father, please help her to go to sleep.*

I had barely walked into the kitchen and begun wiping the counter when Darcy appeared at the doorway again. I gasped. "Darcy, you aren't even trying. Now get back in your bed, right now!" My facial muscles contorted into a fierce scowl. Opening her eyes wide, she turned abruptly and ran into her bedroom crying.

Oh, that girl. Why doesn't she cooperate? I just don't understand why she can't lie still in that bed for even one minute.

Suddenly, the heat of the day and tension in my body swallowed my patience. I couldn't stand it. I rushed into the bedroom and undressed. Beads of sweat clung to my body. I quickly pulled on my bathing suit and ran out to the backyard. I felt like screaming.

I dove into the pool and the cool water cleansed my body of tension and frustration. As I swam several laps, my tears mingled with the water. *Jesus, Jesus, please make Darcy go to sleep. When she doesn't take a nap, she cries and whines. I want to enjoy myself at the party.*

I climbed onto an air mattress and floated peacefully under the cloudless, blue sky. Kicking gently, I guided the raft around the pool, trailing my hands in the refreshing, sparkling water.

My thoughts wandered back to Larry and our discussion at the restaurant. *Lord, why can't I just love and accept Larry as he is? I'm always trying to change him, but it doesn't do any good. I want him to spend more time with me. I want him to talk to me more, but my nagging only pushes him farther away. Jesus, I really believe you want to make him into your kind of man, but it's not happening.*

An inner voice rebuffed me. "My thoughts are not your thoughts, neither are your ways my ways...For as the heavens are higher than the earth, so are my ways higher than your ways, and my thoughts than your thoughts."

Yes, Lord, I recognize those verses from Isaiah 55, but you still aren't doing anything...maybe I'm in the way with all of my nagging. Is that it?

He didn't have to answer me because I knew it was. No matter how hard I tried to have kind, loving communication, invariably negative, pessimistic nagging would win over.

Lord, I just don't feel loved. I know you love me, but... I tried to clarify my thoughts... *but with the way I treat Darcy and Larry, I guess I find it hard to believe you really could love me. Oh, I know about your unconditional love, but I don't feel it.*

Tears trickled down into my wet hair. *Father, I really do want to love Larry and Darcy unconditionally. I just don't seem to know how.*

I paused as if expecting a sermon on love. But instead, three words echoed in my head: Show your love.

Show your love...show your love. The words ricocheted in my mind. I thought of many ways to demonstrate my love but set them aside one by one, hoping for an unusual, spectacular way. Then it occurred to me: *I'll have a surprise birthday party for Larry! I've never done that before. I'll show him how much I love him and he'll have to love me back. Yeah, he'll be so grateful that he'll have to spend more time with me. That's it!*

I paddled over to the side of the pool and jumped out. Wrapping a towel around me, I breezed into the house and down the hall, formulating in my mind the list of people I would invite to Larry's party.

Passing Darcy's room, I glanced in, expecting to find her playing. I stopped. Darcy lay on her bed, surrounded by books...asleep.

Praise you, Lord! Oh, Father, I really appreciate your doing that for me. You showed me your love, now I'm going to show Larry mine.

13

The Party Was a Success, But the Price Was High

June 25

Yes, Claudia, that's right. The party will be this Saturday. I'm glad you received the invitation so soon and can come." I was relieved that Claudia had called to let me know her invitation had arrived safely. I hoped I hadn't forgotten anyone.

Claudia was curious. "Kathy, how are you going to make the party a surprise if you're having it at your house?"

"That's the best part. I had Jim ask Larry to play tennis with him that afternoon at one o'clock. Everyone will arrive at our house at two-thirty, and Jim will bring Larry back at three. Doesn't that sound great? I'm so excited. You know, I've never done anything like this before. I sure hope it works.

"Well, it sounds foolproof to me. I just hope Larry feels like playing tennis that day."

"That's the least of my worries. Larry will play tennis any chance he gets. What he may not like, though, is coming home all sweaty and tired to find twenty people waiting for him."

"I bet he'll love it. Well, I've got to go, but count on us to be there and if you need any help, let me know. Bye."

"Bye, Claudia. Thanks."

Smiling, I hung up the phone. *This is going to be so much fun. I just can't wait to see his face.* In my heart, I counted on this feat to make Larry love me more, but I wouldn't admit it to myself very often. It sounded too selfish.

During the next few days, Darcy really got on my nerves. I had so much to think about and organize, and she seemed to sense my tension, demanding even more attention from me than usual. As I tried to plan the menu, she wanted to play with modeling clay, which I knew would make a big mess. But I also knew that saying no would only elicit persistent begging and possibly a temper tantrum. I was not prepared to handle that, so I relented.

In the meantime, my mind swirled with plans. *I'll make the cake on Friday night while Larry is at work. Sally can keep it at her house until Saturday. But where am I going to hide all the extra food and paper goods? I don't have enough cabinet space in the kitchen.*

I tried to think of all the other places in the house where Larry seldom looked, possible hiding places, and I decided which of those I could use. That made me more confident. I was determined to pull this surprise off, hoping it would make Larry appreciate me more.

On Saturday morning, I could hardly sit still. I tried to keep busy by cleaning the house. But Darcy and Mark, sensing my nervousness, whined and cried for attention all day.

Darcy, please let me get the house clean, I pleaded mentally. The house was beginning to look better and I hoped Larry hadn't noticed my unusually furious pace. Once he left at one o'clock, I would have to put the kids down for their naps, take all the food out, wrap his gift, and get the cake from Sally's house.

Internally, I felt as if I were a rubber band pulled taut to its limit. *Nothing can go wrong. This party has to come off perfectly. Larry will have to love me for this one.*

I flashed back to another surprise I had pulled on Larry when we were first dating in high school. After school one day, when I knew he was practicing with his water polo team at a nearby college, I drove over and walked right into the pool area waving at Larry. He turned crimson as all his friends teased him, because girlfriends never went to practices. I watched from a nearby bench for about twenty minutes, the only spectator around. I was delighted when his buddies needled him for several days after that. Boy, was that fun. After the incident was over, Larry kept telling me I shouldn't do it again, but I could tell by his smile that he halfway enjoyed the attention.

Larry's voice broke through my reverie. "Kathy, Jim's here. We're going now."

"Okay, have a good time," I cried out from the back bedroom. Little did he know what he would be coming home to. Now, it was time to get busy.

Picking up Mark, I walked to his room. I checked his diaper and moaned. It was dirty. I had changed him just thirty minutes before, so I could put him down for his nap without hassle. Taking the opportunity to review mentally my "to-do" list, I pulled a clean diaper out of the drawer and changed him again.

Distracted by thoughts of all the things that still needed to be done, I nervously laid Mark in his crib and shut the door. *Whew, that's one thing settled*, I sighed. But I was only two steps down the hall when I heard Mark start to cry. *That's funny. He usually goes right to sleep.*

I walked back into his room and checked his diaper pins but didn't find anything wrong. I laid him down again. He began to cry immediately. "No, Mark, no. Please don't do this to me. Remember, you're my good baby. Now, go to sleep."

I closed the door, hoping that being out of Mark's sight would stop his crying, but he continued at full volume. *If I get him up, I won't be able to do as much as I would otherwise. He's got to go to sleep.*

I decided to put Darcy down for her nap and wait to see if Mark would stop crying. After I raced through reading a book to her, Darcy wiggled on top of her bed, "Mommy, can we swim later?"

"No, honey, we're going to have company this afternoon. Now, Mommy really needs you to help and go to sleep, okay?"

"Goody, goody. Who's coming over?"

"I don't have time to tell you right now. Sleep tight!"

I almost slammed the door as I hurried out of her room. My heart sank as I heard Mark still screaming. *I can't let him scream like that. It drives me crazy. Maybe I can rock him to sleep.*

While rocking him, I concentrated on all the things I still needed to do. *Oh, no, it's one-thirty. I've got to hurry.*

Mark's alert eyes stared at me. "For heaven's sake, Mark," I whispered, "go to sleep." I rocked faster. I was one blink away from tears as Darcy's door creaked open. Watching her disappear into the kitchen, I sighed. "All right, Lord. I'll just ignore her for now. It's more important that Mark goes to sleep."

The rocking chair squeaked faster, and I tried to sing, but my throat was too tight. Finally, after fifteen minutes, Mark's heavy eyelids closed and I laid him carefully in his crib. *Don't come in now, Darcy. Just stay away.*

Tiptoeing out of the room, I practically ran down the hall wondering where Darcy could be. The minutes were fast disappearing and the guests would start to arrive soon.

I turned the corner into the kitchen. Gasping from shock, I stopped. Darcy sat on the kitchen carpet surrounded by hundreds of tiny pieces of modeling clay. *Oh, no, why did I leave that out on the counter?*

In one stride, I stood towering over Darcy. "Darcy, look what you've done! I've got too many things to do without having to clean up this mess."

I raised my hand and shot it down, slapping Darcy's cheek. She covered her face with her hands and screamed hysterically. *I don't care. She's caused me trouble just when I need all the help I can get. Now nothing will be ready.*

I dropped to my knees, trying to scoop up the muted-gray speckled pieces.

"Darcy, Darcy, can't you do anything right? I told you we're having company."

As I picked up the mess, the slapping sound echoed within me. Guilt replaced my anger. *Oh, no, Father, I've done it again. I wanted everything to be perfect and now I've spoiled it. Look what I've done to Darcy.*

Darcy stared at me as tears continued to roll down her cheeks. As I started to move toward her, she again covered her face. I took a deep breath, then let it out slowly.

"Darcy, I'm sorry. I'm really sorry. Mommy wants to get everything ready for the party and you made a mess. I shouldn't have gotten mad at you though."

I gently pulled her hands down from her face and tried to smile. "C'mon now, please help me get ready; then we'll go over to Sally's house and get Daddy's cake."

Her face brightened. "Cake? Okay."

I looked at the red mark on her cheek that was fading to a dull blush. *Father, I promise never to touch Darcy again in anger. I'm sorry.*

Sniffling back my tears, I grasped Darcy's hand and we went to get the cake. Shortly after we had returned and I had taken out the chips and dips, the guests started to arrive. Several of the women helped me set out the food, and at two-fifty, I stationed one of the men at the window to watch for Jim's car.

At five minutes after three, he yelled, "Here they come!"

Everyone took their preassigned places. They were smiling and giggling excitedly and several kept whispering, "Shhh," making more noise than before.

Suddenly, I remembered the movie camera. I ran down the hall, retrieved the camera, and stood ready.

Larry opened the door. His T-shirt was clinging to his wet skin and his hair was disheveled. He looked tired.

Everyone shouted, "Surprise!" and started singing "Happy birthday to you..."

Larry blinked. He stood with his mouth open, his hand still on the doorknob. He stared as everyone broke into laughter.

Larry's wide-eyed amazement broke into a half-smile. "Oh, no, I can't believe it. You've got to be kidding."

He stepped over to the nearest chair and plopped down. I laid my hand on his shoulder and kissed him. "Happy birthday, sweetheart. I love you."

"Oh, honey, this is fantastic. How did you ever do it?"

"It wasn't easy," I half-joked, knowing the price had been high.

Everyone surrounded Larry and congratulated him on his twenty-eighth birthday. Screeching her delight, Darcy ran over and jumped onto his lap.

Father, thank you that everything went so well— except for my outburst at Darcy.

My heart was heavy. It wasn't the sweet victory I'd imagined. It showed me I wasn't handling stress as well as I thought. I could see that the battle was yet to be won.

14

Love Is a Choice,
Not a Feeling

July 10

"Honey, I just have to thank you again for the wonderful surprise party. That was something else. You really did surprise me." Larry wrapped his arms around me, squeezing tightly.

"I really had a good time planning it," I said, returning his smile. "Just wait until you see the movies of you walking in that door. You won't believe the amazed look on your face."

But Larry's appreciative words weren't what I really wanted. *Had he spent more time with me this week? No! He had been just as consumed by his work as usual. What did I have to do to get his attention anyway? Kill myself?*

When Agnes and Neil's invitation came in the mail a week later inviting us to a neighborhood barbecue, I thought, *this will be Larry's opportunity to show me how appreciative he is.*

"Larry, did you notice Agnes and Neil's invitation to their house for Saturday?" I anxiously inquired.

"Yes, I did. Unfortunately, I've already told Fred I'd work to repay him for a time he worked for me. I'm really sad I have to miss the barbecue."

I turned away in disappointment. *Now, Kathy, don't get upset. He didn't do it on purpose; it just happened. Don't blame him; it's not his fault.*

Even though I realized it wasn't his choice to work, I wanted to blame him.

When Saturday arrived, Larry got ready to leave. Walking over to me, he commented, "Honey, I am really sorry that I can't go to the barbecue with you. It sounds like a lot of fun and I would have enjoyed being with you and the kids."

I stared straight into his eyes. "Really, Larry? Do you mean that? You really would have gone if it hadn't been for your promise to Fred?"

Larry appeared surprised at my intensity. "Of course, Kathy. Don't you think I want to go?"

My mind raced. I didn't want to get into another argument. How could I share my feelings without complaining?

"Well, it's just that I miss you so much and it seems like— you'll notice, I said seems like—every time there is something to do, you have to work. I just wonder sometimes if you even want to be with me and the kids."

Larry's hazel eyes softened. "I'm sorry I give you that impression. But I assure you I really do want to be with you. As soon as we get on our feet financially, I'll have more time to spend with you. I promise."

For the first time, I believed him. He really did want to be with us. I decided I would stop complaining and trust his love for me from now on.

A couple of hours later, Darcy, Mark, and I walked over to Agnes and Neil's backyard where several families mingled. Agnes had prepared four large salads and the barbeque coals were white-hot, ready to cook the hamburgers and hot dogs.

Several of the neighbors sat in groups visiting, while children ran back and forth chasing balls and playing with the dog.

"Wow, Agnes, this is really special. But I still can't believe you wouldn't let me bring any food."

Agnes grinned. "Well, we just wanted everyone to come, have a good time, and not worry about anything."

"That's really sweet of you. Looks like you've got a good turnout."

I scanned the back yard. Noticing Pat and Sally talking together, I walked over to them. Darcy trailed behind me, fearfully eyeing the dog, and Mark took in the view as I balanced him on my hip.

Once Darcy became acquainted with the dog, she raced around with the other children. I watched her play. She looked so darling in her clean, green-and-white-checked shorts outfit. Her short, blonde hair actually looked as if it were starting to get thicker. She was growing up so fast.

When it was time to eat, I prepared our plates and sat down beside Ted, one of our neighbors. Moving over on the picnic bench to make room for us, he helped me set down the glasses of punch.

Darcy eagerly began eating her hot dog. All her running around had made her ravenously hungry.

Ted leaned toward Darcy, brushing her bangs back from her sweaty forehead. "Darcy, you're such a good little girl," he remarked.

Pride welled up within me. "Yes, Darcy is a good little girl. Although she does sometimes remind me of the little girl in the nursery rhyme who when she was good was very, very good, but when she was bad, she was horrid."

Ted laughed.

"Darcy's my special little girl." I hugged her, kissing her on the top of her head. The love I felt at that moment almost made tears come to my eyes. *I really do love you. Darcy,* I whispered in my mind.

But by the time I had thought the words, confusion and guilt surrounded the warm feelings of love and suffocated them. Guilt snickered, "How can you say you love her when you treat her so badly?" Confusion poked, "What kind of love hits and kicks and slaps and..."

Trying to divert my attention, I turned to Ted. "I hear you landed a new job. How's it going?"

As Ted raved about his higher-paying position, my imagination continued its dialogue. *I'm trying. I'm trying. I do love Darcy.*

"When she's good," the voice answered back. "What kind of love is that?"

Why do I hate her so much when she's naughty? I probed. *Can love exist alongside hate?*

Then I remembered a concept I had learned many years before: *Love is a choice for the highest good of the person.*

That's the answer. *Love is a choice, not a feeling. I do love Darcy. I just have to learn to express my love in choices for her good.*

The condemning voices seemed to retreat. I remembered the many ways I had hurt Darcy, and as Ted continued to talk about his new job, I reassured myself: *I am doing better. I'm not getting angry as often. God is working. I just have to continue to trust Him. And that's that!*

Later that afternoon, several of the women and I sat around a picnic table talking. Mary, a friend from my Bible study, asked, "Kathy, how are you doing controlling your anger?"

"Well...," I forced a smile, but my face grew hot. "I have my ups and downs. I guess I have the hardest times when Darcy makes mistakes. She does so many dumb things."

"Kathy, I think that's because she's a child," Julie, another friend from Bible study, spoke up.

"Yeah, I know that," I replied, "but it's so aggravating."

"I agree, Kathy," Mary said. "I did something once that helped me along those lines. Using the information I found in a child development book, I made a list of everything a child Jeremy's age might do, like spill milk, or not pick up his toys, or not share—things like that. I put the list on the refrigerator and each time he did one of them, instead of getting angry, I would put a check beside it. That really helped me to remember that his immaturity caused him to act the way he did. He wasn't doing it on purpose."

Everyone murmured their approval.

"Wow, Mary, that's a great idea. I'm going to do that." I mentally made a note to make myself a list the first chance I got.

The conversation continued and Anne began saying how thrilled she was that she had finally potty trained her two-and-a-half-year-old daughter. She raved about how nice it was not to have to wash diapers or change her daughter.

Anne's news made me think about Darcy. It had been several months since I had put Darcy back in diapers. She was over two-and-a-half now; maybe she was ready. It sure would be nice to have to change only Mark. And the summer months were supposed to be the easiest time to try because she'd be able to run around in just her training pants.

I went home from the barbecue trying to decide if I should try potty training Darcy again. "Well," I assured myself, "if she doesn't respond right away or if I can't handle it, I can always quit. I'm going to do it."

When I made a list of things Darcy could be expected to do, I added, "Have lots of potty training accidents."

The next day, I dressed Darcy only in her training pants and reintroduced her to the potty chair. I hoped this time would be successful.

15

It's a Growth Process —
For My Child *and* Me

August 1

I glanced at the many rows of book racks and was amazed. This Christian bookstore had added a lot of books and items since I had last been there. How was I ever going to choose a book for Alice, my neighbor, to read in the hospital?

Then, a title in the family section caught my eye. Picking up the book, I read the title *Understanding the Male Temperament* by Tim LaHaye.[1] I laughed. *Boy, could I stand to learn about Larry's temperament.* The more I looked through it, the more interested I became.

Maybe if I understood Larry, I wouldn't always be trying to change him. I decided I would buy it, along with something else for Alice.

When I finally found a book I thought she would enjoy, I paid for both, and drove home, hoping Darcy and Mark would cooperate and let me read later on.

When they both went down for their naps easily, I praised the Lord. Now I could start my book. Two hours later, I was still reading and was amazed that the children were still asleep. Fascinated, I read about the four different temperaments that Dr. LaHaye described. I identified Larry's temperament — and mine. *No wonder he reacts the way he does. And no wonder I react the way I do. I've always known Larry doesn't look at things the same way I do, but I've never understood why. Now I know.*

For the next couple of days, I read during every spare moment I had. I began to understand that my *melancholy* temperament was based on perfectionism. For the first time, I acknowledged that I did tend to be a perfectionist. I had never recognized that in myself before. Maybe these perfectionist tendencies were what made me so impatient and demanding of Darcy. I decided to keep an eye on myself and see if it influenced the way I treated her.

Toward the end of the book, there was a section called "How to Cure Anger, Bitterness, or Resentment." I wondered if following its seven steps could help me. A spark of hope lit within my heart as I read the section. *Was this the real reason the Lord had me buy this book?*

Step number one was: "Face your anger as sin." While I believe that not all anger is sin, I knew that my uncontrollable anger was a habit in my life that often controlled me, taking over my thoughts and actions. That was wrong. *Okay, Father,* I prayed, *I'm going to start off on the right foot by telling you that I agree that my particular anger habit is wrong, that it is sin. And I ask you to forgive me.* (See Appendix I - How to Deal with Anger.)

All right, then, what was step two? "Confess every angry thought or deed as soon as it occurs." That was interesting. Maybe the cause of my anger was really internal—my thoughts and perceptions. I recalled the last few times in which I was out of control. Every time had started with not trusting the Lord for the circumstances I was in. Then I became worried or tense and these feelings turned into anger. *Lord, I ask you to help me recognize when I'm starting to think negatively or angrily.*

"Ask God to take away this angry pattern," was step three. *Okay, I will. Father, I ask you to take away my angry thought pattern. Even as I ask you, though, my faith is weak. How can I ask so simply for such a complicated thing? Please help my unbelief.*

Step four was: "Forgive the person who has caused your anger." Darcy! Larry! These were the two people with whom

I was most often angry. But forgive them? I was the one who needed the forgiveness. I was the one who was in the wrong. But I knew that I didn't totally believe that. I believed Larry didn't spend enough time with me or have the right priorities. And Darcy demanded too much of my time and energy—too much of me. I was bitter toward them and that was at the root of my problem. I had never been honest with myself before, because I knew as a Christian I shouldn't be bitter.

All right, Lord, I ask you to forgive me for my bitterness and help me to forgive Darcy and Larry. I know you are using them in my life to make me a more godly woman. I just keep taking the mass of clay from which I am molded off your potter's wheel. Help me to stay there from now on.

"Formally give thanks for anything that bothers you," spelled out number five. Why, it might take all day to follow through on this step. Everything bothered me: Darcy's wet and dirty training pants, raisins in the rug, Larry's working long hours, the dripping faucet...

As I mentally listed annoying situations, I realized these were the circumstances that flamed my anger. These were the potentially dangerous situations of which I needed to be careful.

I jumped up from the sofa and retrieved a piece of paper and a pencil. I wrote down all of my frustrations and tacked my list next to Darcy's list.

Returning to the couch, I read the sixth step, "Think only good, wholesome, and positive thoughts." I knew this would be difficult for me. I tended to look at the negative side of things and found it hard to focus on God's joy when circumstances weren't going my way. I wondered how I could combat that. Then I remembered someone telling me about a "blessings list" they had made. Maybe if I made a list of blessings, I could refer to it when I was thinking negatively.

Another list? This was getting to be ridiculous. But I

knew it could help, so I started writing. Then minutes later, I was surprised at how many blessings I had thought of. My heart felt bubbly with thanksgiving.

After I put my blessings list on the refrigerator, next to the others, I picked up the book again. Step seven: "Repeat the above formula each time you are angry." Now I understood. This wasn't just a one time thing, it was a process. I should follow this whole formula, step by step, every time I became angry. I could see it was definitely going to be a challenge to put the steps into practice.

But I finished the section and decided I would give Dr. LaHaye's method a try, allowing the Lord to cure me of my dreaded "disease"—uncontrolled anger—which I knew was eating my heart out and destroying my life.

I wondered how I could make sure I followed the seven steps. Often, in the past, I had said I would try something and then would forget all about it. Thinking of my other lists, I decided I'd copy the seven steps down on a card and tape it to the window above my kitchen sink. That way I could memorize them and be reminded to use them.

I found a large, lined card in my desk, wrote the steps down, and taped it to the window. *Oh, Lord, please help me follow them. And help me get back to disciplining Darcy consistently. That helped me so much before. Maybe, if I am faithful to both of these projects, I really will see victory. Jesus, I've got to. I don't know how much longer I can go on like this without doing something really destructive. I'll depend on you to remind me often.*

At that moment, He told me what to do: "Put verses about anger throughout the house."

That's a good idea, Lord. I fished out more cards from the desk, wrote down verses on them, and taped them in prominent places in the rooms I went into most often.

Now when I washed the dishes or fixed meals, I read the seven steps again and again until I had them memorized.

When I led Darcy to the bathroom after a potty training

accident, I studied the card on the mirror. "Let all bitterness and wrath and anger and clamor and slander be put away from you, along with all malice. And be kind to one another, tender-hearted, forgiving each other, just as God in Christ also has forgiven you" (Ephesians 4:31-32).

In the kitchen, when I retrieved the spoon to discipline Darcy, I saw, "Hatred stirs up strife; but love covers all transgressions" (Proverbs 10:12).

In Darcy's room, I put, "A hot-tempered man stirs up strife; but the slow to anger pacifies contention" (Proverbs 15:18).

When I noticed myself starting to think negatively or complain about my life, I would pick several blessings and praise God for them. The check marks were lining up rapidly beside Darcy's mistakes, but instead of becoming angry, I understood they were a part of her growth process.

Everywhere I turned, God reminded me He could help me control my anger. Although the flame of hope was strong within me, I still had occasional, flickering doubts about the true possibility of victory.

Note:
1. Dr. Tim LaHaye, *Understanding the Male Temperament* (Old Tappan, NY: Fleming H. Revell, 1979).

16

Success Happens One Day at a Time

August 30

My blurry mind struggled to wake up as I focused my eyes on the clock and read 8:04. Snapping alert, I listened for the children but didn't hear a sound. Evidently, Darcy and Mark weren't awake yet. I was surprised. Remembering today was Wednesday and I had a La Leche League meeting to go to at nine-thirty, I realized I needed to hurry.

As I dressed, I heard Darcy playing in her room and Mark babbling in his crib. Even though I started to feel rushed, I was happy. The past two weeks had gone smoothly. By repeating the seven steps, I had been able to catch myself almost every time my anger had started to erupt.

Darcy ran into my bedroom. "Mommy, what we having for breakfast?"

"Oatmeal and toast," I replied, putting on my sandals.

"I want pancakes. Pancakes, please, Mommy."

"No, Darcy, we had pancakes yesterday. I don't want you to have too much syrup."

Darcy's face puckered up into a tearless cry.

Rushing past her into Mark's room, I began dressing him. I heard Darcy screaming in my bedroom; my chest and throat tightened. *Oh, Lord, I don't need her to have a temper tantrum when we're in a hurry. But step number five says to give thanks for anything that bothers me, so thank you that Darcy is having a fit.* I smiled. *This is almost comical. Here I am changing Mark's dirty diaper and being grateful that Darcy is screaming in the next room.*

Mark lay on his back on the changing table sucking his fist. His round, chubby belly wiggled as I wiped off his bottom. Just then, the phone rang. I picked up Mark's naked body and raced to answer it. It was Claudia asking for a ride to the La Leche League meeting. I assured her I could be at her house at nine-fifteen. When she continued to talk, I sighed helplessly. How could I tactfully get her to hang up? But within a few minutes she finished. I hung up the phone and noticed it was eight-thirty.

By the time we ate breakfast and I dressed Darcy, it was nine o'clock. I hadn't even packed Mark's diaper bag yet. My tension increased as Darcy asked question after question, and to make things worse, I couldn't find my keys.

When I had finally packed the bag and found my keys, I was perspiring and gritting my teeth. I strapped Mark into his car seat and reached for Darcy. I felt something wet. *Oh, no, it can't be. Not now, when we're late.*

"Darcy, are your pants wet?" Her frightened face stared at me. "You've been doing so well. Why did you pick this morning to have an accident?"

I gripped her arm tightly and pulled her into the house. Her little legs struggled to keep up. "Honestly, Darcy, why now? Are you doing this on purpose?"

My tension turned to fury. "Now we'll be late and Claudia is waiting for us." I continued to spew out my frustration.

As I grappled to pull down Darcy's training pants, I noticed the verse on the mirror. "Let all bitterness and wrath..." *I don't care about that. She's doing this on purpose. She's got to be. She's been doing so well the last couple of weeks.*

Inside, I was jumping up and down. Tension-building thoughts raced through my mind: *I'm going to be late... Claudia is waiting...*I jerked my hand back and let it slam against Darcy's wet bottom.

"Next time you better tell me first," I yelled. By the time I had spanked Darcy five times, shame replaced my anger.

I escaped into Darcy's room searching for another pair of training pants. Returning to the bathroom, I sensed guilt and failure overwhelming me. "See, Darcy, that's what happens when you wet your pants," I defended myself. But inside, I cried out, *Oh, no, I've done it again. I can't believe it. I've been doing so well and now I've blown it!*

I picked up Darcy and carried her out to the car. Tears tumbled down my face as I drove the car out of the garage. *Dear Jesus, I'm so ashamed. When am I ever going to learn? When am I ever going to get complete control? Do I have to practice the seven steps again?*

At first, I didn't want to go through them. Then I remembered how much I had learned in the last couple of weeks. When I had followed the seven steps, I had sensed a renewing, cleansing power that enabled me to control myself during each aggravating situation.

All right, Lord, here I go again. Father, I confess my outburst and spanking Darcy in uncontrolled anger as sin. I ask you to forgive me and to cleanse me even though I don't deserve it.

I turned to Darcy but couldn't look into her eyes. Embarrassed, I asked, "Darcy, will you forgive me for getting angry with you?"

Darcy's tear-stained face gazed at me uncomprehendingly. I knew she didn't know what forgive meant, but I needed to ask for her forgiveness anyway. Many times in the past weeks, I had consciously not become angry so that I wouldn't have to ask for her forgiveness.

Focusing on the Lord again, I prayed, *Jesus, I forgive Darcy for having an accident. Help me to remember that she doesn't do it on purpose, that she's still learning. Thank you that Darcy's accidents are helping me control my anger habit. It seems like it's taking a long time but I know I'm in the process of learning, too.*

I looked into the rearview mirror to wipe my face. Then I

wiped off Darcy's. We pulled into Claudia's driveway and she got into the car with her two-year-old daughter.

Hoping I didn't look too upset, I tried, but found it hard, to share Claudia's excitement over her daughter's latest accomplishments.

When we arrived at the park where our August meeting was always held, I hurriedly set out the books and items I sold as treasurer. The meeting began. I sat down on a blanket with Darcy in my lap and Mark lying next to me. As a regular part of the meeting everyone shared stories about their month, and this time most of the women talked about how great they thought it was to be a mother.

Guilt plundered my heart of peace and joy. It screamed within me, *What a terrible mother you are. You beat your kid and nobody else does.*

No, no, I argued. *God has forgiven me. He's forgotten about it and I'm cleansed.*

Then guilt reared its ugly head once again, *How can you call yourself a Christian the way you act?*

I'm not perfect, but I'm becoming more like my Savior, Jesus Christ.

When it was my turn to share, I mumbled something about how Mark was starting to eat different kinds of foods. But all the while I wondered, *Don't any of them get angry sometimes? Will I ever have complete victory? Does God still love me even though I've failed Him? Why don't I experience the joys of motherhood?*

After everyone shared, Darcy played with the other children while I sold books and baby food grinders. It was close to lunchtime when I dropped Claudia off at her house. Darcy whined complaints about being hungry, but I tried to tune them out.

Think positive! Think positive! I began singing "Jesus loves me..." and Darcy joined in. With a sigh of relief, I drove into our garage, unloaded everyone and everything into the house, and promptly fixed lunch.

As I thought about the morning, I tried to encourage

myself. *I failed, but at least I'm not failing as often. Most of the time I'm able to catch myself before I'm out of control. I guess it's just going to take more time.*

In the next month, I coped with stressful situations better than I ever had before. When Mark came down with another cold and was coughing throughout the nights, I napped every afternoon and regularly reviewed the seven steps.

Then I came down with Mark's cold. Although my body was weak and easily irritated, I monitored my thoughts carefully to prevent negative thinking from capturing my mind.

I continued to discipline Darcy consistently with the spoon, and eventually her misbehavior was slightly reduced. Her third birthday was coming soon, so I hoped she was growing out of the "terrible twos."

Little by little, like grains of sand dropping through an hourglass, I was seeing victories mount up in a pile. God was working, and for the first time I knew that some day I was going to be in control of my anger. Now when people complimented me on my patience with Darcy in public, I could smile and say thank you instead of mentally rejecting their praise. Maybe I wasn't such a bad mother after all.

17

God Loves Me and So Do I!

September 15

Picking up the phone, I answered, "Hello."

The woman's voice on the other end of the line asked, "Is Kathy Miller home, please?"

"This is she."

"Kathy, this is Joy from the Christian Women's Club. We've noticed how regularly you've been coming to the monthly luncheons and wonder whether you'd consider serving as Nursery Chairman on our new board that begins in October. We'd really love to have you serve the Lord with us."

Surprised, I inquired, "What would the position entail?"

"It means you would attend the luncheons to collect the money for the babysitters and also come to the two other board meetings we have each month."

"Oh, I see." I was flattered that they wanted me to join their board, but I knew I couldn't agree to that kind of a commitment with all the other things I had to do. I also knew what Larry would say if I took on another responsibility.

"Well," I answered, "I'm really glad you thought of me. But ...uh, I really don't think I could at this time. My son, who is only nine months old, is still nursing, so it's hard for me to leave him for very long. And I'm an officer in an organization called La Leche League, which takes some of my time. So I don't think I could. But I really do appreciate your asking me. I enjoy the luncheons so much and you women certainly do a great job of putting them together."

Joy's disappointed voice replied, "I'm sorry that it won't work out now, but do keep us in mind for the future."

We said good-bye and hung up.

I smiled as I thought about Joy's offer. It would be exciting to be involved in something that brings women closer to Christ. But I really did have too much to do already and it would be hard on Mark to leave him so often. Even though he was eating more solid foods, he was not ready to wean yet. Besides, I wanted to continue being treasurer for La Leche League for at least another year. I enjoyed it so much. No, it just wasn't the right time.

The peace in my heart confirmed my decision. But within a few days, the thought of joining the board resurfaced. I began to think about how great it would be to work with a group of Christian women. But, no, I decided it just wasn't possible right now.

It was easy to bury the idea in the "not now, maybe next year" cubbyhole of my mind, as I thought about the responsibilities of my family, La Leche League, Bible study, and maintaining my patience. I didn't need any new pressures in my life. I was sailing along fairly well now, seldom losing control. I didn't want anything to complicate my life.

But as soon as I thought the idea had been safely stashed away, it resurfaced. And like a woman falling in love with a man she used to dislike, it became more attractive each time it emerged.

In the following week, my desire to continue as treasurer for La Leche League dwindled. I had enjoyed the role for two-and-a-half years and now my love for it was slowly disappearing. I was amazed. Each time I thought about the board position, I became excited and drawn to the idea. This was silly, I told myself. I had already told them no. Most likely they had already found someone else. I tried to forget about the possibility.

That Friday, while my friend Karen was visiting with her

two children, the phone rang. It was a woman who introduced herself as Virginia. She was from the same Christian Women's Club.

"Kathy, we on the nominating committee were wondering if by any chance you'd thought any more about joining us as Nursery Chairman. The Lord hasn't filled that position yet. Is He keeping it open for you?"

Unable to restrain myself, I giggled. "Well, as a matter of fact, I have been thinking about it, but I assumed the position would be filled already. I don't know what to say. Can I call you back in a few days after I've prayed about it and have talked with my husband?"

She agreed that would be just fine and left me her number.

My heart raced with joy as I hung up the phone and explained to Karen what had happened. She laughed. "It sure looks like the Lord wants you to join the board, doesn't it?"

"Boy, it sure does. But I don't know what Larry will say. He always says I have enough to do. Even if I quit the treasurer's job, the board position requires more time and responsibility. And what about Mark? How can I leave him?"

"Well," Karen smiled. "If the Lord wants you to do it, He'll show you the way."

The rest of the day I felt excited, yet a little apprehensive, about talking with Larry. How could I ask him in such a way that he might say yes? *Lord, you're going to have to work with me on this one.*

The next morning after Larry finished breakfast, I sat at the table with him. I explained how both Joy and Virginia had called and asked me to be on the board, and how I had increasingly sensed the Lord changing my desires from the treasurer's job to the board position.

Taking a deep breath, I asked, "Honey, what do you think about my joining the board as Nursery Chairman?"

He stared at the hanging Tiffany-styled lamp above us.

Barely breathing, I waited and prayed, *Lord, guide him according to your will. I really want to join the board... please.*

Larry turned to me. "You really think this is what the Lord wants you to do?"

"Yes, I do. I was so sure I would stay treasurer for quite a while longer but He's certainly changed my desires."

"Then I guess it will be all right with me."

Bursting with joy, I exclaimed within, *Thank you, Jesus, thank you. You want me to do it.*

"Larry," I grinned and kissed him, "I'm so glad you said that. I'm so excited."

I immediately reached for the phone on the wall. My hand shook as I dialed Virginia's number, but the happiness she expressed after hearing my answer was reassuring.

Then I called my La Leche League leader to let her know I would be resigning as treasurer. She said she was sorry to hear it but told me not to worry. There were several women who were interested, so she knew it wouldn't be difficult to find a replacement.

For the rest of the day, I anticipated how my first board meeting would go. October fifth was only two weeks away.

During the next week, I prepared the books for the new treasurer of La Leche League. As I finished totaling some figures, my pen ran out of ink. I stared at it in amazement. *This is the pen I've been using for the two-and-a-half years I've been treasurer. How interesting that it should run out of ink the last time I write with it as treasurer.*

The following week, Mark suddenly started to balk at nursing. I couldn't imagine why he wouldn't nurse. His gums were bothering him a little from teething, but I didn't think that would prevent him from nursing altogether. He was becoming a lot more interested in food and he loved drinking from a cup, but I had expected him to nurse at least as long as I had nursed Darcy—fifteen months. However, each time I tried to nurse Mark, he refused.

One day, as I stood at the kitchen sink washing the

dishes, an understanding of all that was happening broke through to my soul like the sun bursting through the clouds after a storm. *Why, of course! With Mark no longer nursing, I'll be able to attend the board meetings and not worry about him being hungry. And my pen running out of ink...it all means God is guiding me.*

Thank you, Jesus. You are doing all this for me, aren't you? I can't believe it. You're showing me over and over again that you are specifically leading me. Your hand is directly upon me. Even though I've hurt Darcy and I'm not in complete control yet, you still love me. I'm important to you and you accept me as I am.

Tears brimmed in my eyes, then plopped into the sudsy dishwater. The realization of God's love for me was overwhelming. "God loves me...again!" I cried out loud, hesitantly mouthing the word "again."

He had never stopped loving me, but the light of that fact had been dissipated in my heart by the anger and low self-esteem I had been nurturing. Now the full strength of that light dispersed all the gloom.

I love you, Lord. I love you so very much! Astonished, I paused in thought. *I haven't told God I love Him for so long. It's been such a long time since I've felt loved by Him and felt loving toward Him. But now I want to shout it from the rooftops. God has shown me how much He loves me and I love Him, too! He wants me to serve Him; He wants to guide me; He wants to love me!*

I couldn't wipe the joyous smile off my face for a week—and I didn't want to. Darcy's temper tantrums didn't bother me. *God loves me!* Mark's teething fussiness didn't faze me. *God cares for me!* The messy house didn't overwhelm me. *God is guiding me!*

Larry couldn't believe the change he saw in me. When he asked why I was so happy, I exclaimed, "Honey, God loves me. He's shown me how much He loves me!"

Larry's quizzical look didn't dilute my joy. "But I thought you knew He loved you!"

"Yes, but I had lost the joy of His love, of realizing He specifically loves me and cares about my life. He has guided me to join the board. Everything that has happened—your allowing me to join the board, my pen running out of ink, Mark's suddenly weaning himself—it all points to God's moving in my life. I'm important to Him."

Larry laughed. "Well, I'm glad it has meant so much to you. That's great!"

Oh, it was great! I sensed that a new chapter was beginning in my life. A chapter entitled "God loves me and so do I!"

18

On My Way to Victory

October 15

Three years old. *I can't believe it.* Darcy turned three on October twelfth. I smiled at her while she sat on the floor watching TV. *Oh, Father, thank you for this last month. It has been glorious. I've rarely been out of control, but more importantly, I love you and I love myself. I know now that I'll never go back to my old angry habit.*

I looked again at my list of things to do in preparation for the family birthday party we were having for Darcy that night. I was relieved that it was a Saturday so that Larry could be here to help me. As soon as he arrived home from his real estate appointment, he could set up the tables and chairs and stay with the kids while I did some last-minute shopping.

Suddenly, I remembered I'd forgotten to tell him I needed his help that afternoon. But I was sure that he didn't have anything else to do, so I expected him home sometime around one o'clock.

As I stirred the cake mix, I glanced at the clock. "Okay, Darcy," I called, "it's ten o'clock, time to turn off the television. That's enough cartoons for this morning."

She frowned. "Mommy, can I watch TV longer, please?"

Well, she's the birthday girl so maybe she can. Oh, wait, when I've let her watch TV longer in the past, it's been twice as hard to get her to turn it off the next day. No, it'll be better if I remain firm on my rule.

"No, sweetie. There are lots of other things you can do.

Why not get out the new toys you got from your birthday party the other day? Your new dolly will be lots of fun to play with."

Pouting, Darcy dramatically turned off the television. I stifled a laugh. She would be a good actress some day.

After she skipped down the hall toward her bedroom, I finished mixing the cake and put it in the oven. I wished I had done more things the day before, but my battle with the flu had made me weak. I looked around and decided I still needed to clean the range, mop the bathroom floor, dust, and vacuum.

I retrieved the vacuum from the hall closet and passed Mark crawling toward his yarn ball. "Hey, Mark, you're really going to town with your crawling, aren't you?" Reaching down, I picked up the soft, multicolored yarn ball and tossed it out in front of him. With a squeal, he crawled toward it.

The phone rang. It was my sister asking for some ideas for a birthday gift for Darcy. Then we started talking about other things, and before I knew it twenty minutes had passed.

Hanging up the phone, I dashed down the hall, looking in each room for Darcy and Mark. I finally found Darcy enthralled in front of the television set watching cartoons. Mark sat nearby trying to stack blocks. I pushed the off button on the TV. Startled, Darcy looked up and began to cry.

"Darcy, I told you, no more television."

I turned on my heels and fetched the vacuum again. Quickly plugging it in, I began vacuuming in the living room. In the adjacent family room, I could see Darcy pounding her fists on the floor. Icy chills traveled down my back, and my chest muscles tensed.

When are these temper tantrums ever going to stop? I thought she'd be over the "terrible twos" by now. Thank heaven the tantrums don't come as often as they used to.

I tried to ignore her and thankfully remembered that Larry would be home soon.

By the time I finished vacuuming the rest of the house, it was eleven-thirty. Walking toward the family room to check on Darcy, I heard the TV.

Again! Won't that girl ever learn? I had had just about enough of this. She was going to learn once and for all. The icy chills I had sensed before blazed into hot flames of wrath.

Passing through the kitchen, I noticed the card with the seven steps tacked on the window. I stopped, took a deep breath, and exhaled slowly. *All right, Kathy, calm down. Yes, Darcy disobeyed, but she's only a little girl. You're not perfect yet and neither is she. Your anger is not going to make her obey. Jesus still has to discipline you and you will have to continue to discipline Darcy. So you might as well get used to it.*

I pulled the wooden spoon out of the drawer. Moving toward Darcy, I prayed, "Lord, thank you for reminding me. Thank you that you're smoothing Darcy's and my own rough edges so that we might become beautiful diamonds sparkling to the praise of your glory."

I turned off the television. As soon as Darcy saw the spoon, her mouth dropped open. "No more TV, Mommy. I promise. No spanking, please?"

"Yes, Darcy, I do have to spank you so that you'll remember next time not to turn on the television."

After swatting Darcy on her bottom three times, I cuddled her as we talked about how important it was for her to obey me. Then we started talking about her birthday party. She quickly recovered from her crying and her face brightened at the prospect of cake and gifts.

"Darcy," I pleaded, "Mommy really needs your help. I have a lot to do to get ready for your party. Can you play nicely while I dust, and then it will be time for lunch, okay?"

Darcy nodded. She jumped off my lap and ran into her

room. I heard her fishing several toys out of her overflowing toy box.

Feeling relieved, I put Mark in his playpen and dusted the living room furniture. As I thought about all the other projects I had wanted to accomplish that day, I grimaced. I was just going to have to settle for whatever I could get done. It wouldn't matter that much if the house wasn't spotless.

I reminded myself about the perfectionist tendencies I was discovering within myself. I had been recognizing my "all or nothing" attitude: If everything wasn't done, I couldn't be satisfied. Now I was learning to be content with whatever I could accomplish. It was just as pleasing and less stressful.

Sighing in resignation, I finished dusting the bedrooms and heard my stomach rumble with hunger. It was time for lunch.

We finished lunch without hassle and by one-thirty, Darcy and Mark were down for their naps. Sitting near the front window, I expected to see Larry's car drive up at any moment. I decided to read a magazine since Larry would be home soon. I finished reading an article, but he still had not returned. Finally, I decided that I needed to get back to work, even if Larry wasn't home yet.

As I took my china out of the cupboard, I found myself fuming inside. *Now, why is he late? He must know we have a lot to do to get ready for the party. I can't set up that heavy table all by myself. Where is he?*

My anticipation evolved into anger during the next hour. Realizing that stress was choking out my trust in the Lord's timing, I often paused to quote some verses on anger. I sensed temporary relief and thanked the Lord. But when Larry still didn't arrive, the tension returned.

Father, please make him come home soon. There is too much for me to do alone. And please help me with this anger I feel. I've really been trying to control my emotions. And I don't want to make Larry feel guilty when he comes home. Right now, I submit to your plan and timetable for today. I thank you that you are in control and that I can trust you. Everything that you want to get done will get done.

I felt peace wash away my anger and tension. It was so exciting to see the Lord helping me again. It seemed that His immediate peace was always available as soon as I relaxed in His control. I had experienced it happening over and over again.

Suddenly, I heard the sound of the garage door moving and the hum of the car. "Lord, thank you that you're helping me to have the right attitude."

Larry rushed into the bedroom where I was doing some last-minute chores. "Hi, Kathy. I'm sorry I'm late but I went by Bob's for a minute. He's still pretty sick even though he's doing a little better now. He might be able to come back to work in about a month."

I expected my anger to return, but instead I sensed the Lord's peace. "I'm so glad he's doing better," I replied. "That was thoughtful of you to visit him."

"I've been meaning to get over to see him for a long time and decided I'd better stop putting it off and do it today."

Setting his keys down on top of the bureau, he turned to face me. His dark hair and hazel eyes appeared especially handsome to me.

He grasped my hands and pulled me down with him onto the bed. "You know what? I sure do appreciate you." He wrapped his arms around me.

I tried to pout but giggled instead. "You do, huh? I don't know if I appreciate you. I wanted you to come right home so that you could help me get everything ready for the birthday party tonight."

Larry began to pull away his arms but I held them around me.

"It's my fault, don't worry," I interjected. "I didn't tell you. I thought you'd realize it. Don't get me wrong; I'm glad you went to see Bob, but I sure was getting angry when you were late."

"Honey, I can't read your mind. You've got to tell me these things; otherwise I don't know. Of course I'll help you." He started to get up but I pulled him back.

"Larry," I paused, clarifying my thoughts, "I realize that I do expect you to be a mind reader. I'm always thinking you should automatically know my needs and then meet them. I've got to start sharing them with you more."

"So start now." Larry gazed intently into my eyes.

I diverted my eyes from his and smoothed back his hair from his forehead. "Well, I guess one of my needs these days is for more attention. Unfortunately, when I've tried to tell you that in the past, I haven't been able to do it without making you feel guilty for being gone so much." I stared into his eyes. "So let me change my appeal a little by requesting that we talk more when you're home. Maybe somehow we can have more time to communicate and air our feelings. Sometimes I feel so alone. With everyone else's husband home in the evenings, I really start to feel cheated."

"Kathy, I can understand how that could happen. From now on we'll try to talk more. Maybe we won't turn on the television so soon after the kids have gone to bed. How does that sound?"

"That would be fantastic!" I leaned over and kissed him.

I jumped up from the bed laughing. "And now I request we get ready for Darcy's third birthday party. Let's go!"

Grabbing his arm, I pulled him up in mock strength. After I told him what things still needed to be done, I left to finish my shopping.

That evening, Darcy had a great time at her birthday party. Everything wasn't perfect like I had intended, but she didn't notice and neither did anyone else. Yet more important to me was my calm and peaceful attitude. I still wasn't perfect, but, at least, I was becoming more content and getting a handle on my anger. I was on my way to victory.

19

A New Love for My Child

November 15

Mother and I relaxed on my living room couch planning Thanksgiving dinner, which was only a week away. Darcy handed me her doll to dress and then brought in a game to play.

"Well, Kathy," my mother laughed, "you might as well find something we can all do together. Darcy doesn't want to be left out."

"Yeah, I guess you're right. At least it's not too long until her bedtime. Darcy, would you like us to play ball with you?" I reasoned that Mother and I would still be able to talk while rolling a ball back and forth.

"Yes, yes, let's play ball," Darcy cheered. She ran to her bedroom and returned with her red plastic ball.

"Darcy," I explained. "Grandma and I will roll it on the carpet and you can jump over it."

"Okay." Darcy's eyes brightened in delight.

I positioned myself on the floor, a few feet away from my mother. We rolled the ball back and forth and continued to plan the dinner. Each time it rolled across, Darcy took careful aim and jumped over it.

"Now, what will we serve for dessert?" my mother asked.

"How about our customary pumpkin pie and..." I began. Then I gasped in horror as I saw Darcy jump on top of the ball. Her feet flew out from beneath her and with a sickening thud, the back of her head slammed down onto the carpet. I froze.

Mother reached over and cradled Darcy's rigid body in

her arms. A moment later, Darcy's body fell limp and her head dangled over my mother's arm.

"Oh, no, Mother, she's unconscious," I yelled.

Mother started slapping Darcy's face, calling, "Darcy, Darcy, wake up."

I jumped to my feet. "I'm going to call the paramedics." I ran to the phone in the family room and picked up the receiver with my trembling hands.

"Kathy," my mother shouted, "Darcy's conscious again."

I put the receiver back and ran to the living room. Darcy's eyes were open but she looked dazed. I knelt beside her and cupped her face in my hands. "Darcy, how do you feel?"

Her eyes tried to focus on me and her head wobbled in my hands. "My head hurts." She lifted her hand to touch her head.

"Okay, honey. It's bound to hurt considering how hard you hit it." I took her in my arms and sat down on the couch.

Mother and I sat there for a while discussing what we should do. Soon, Darcy complained, "Mommy, my tummy feels sick. I want to go to sleep."

I tried to smile but my lips felt heavy. "That's the first time in her whole life she's volunteered to go to sleep. Mother, I'm going to call our clinic and see what they say."

I lifted Darcy onto my mother's lap. When I reached the nurse on the phone, I told her what had happened. She suggested I take Darcy to the nearest emergency room. Then I dialed Larry at work and he said he would meet us at the hospital.

Mother stayed with Mark and within minutes I was carrying sleeping Darcy into the hospital. After I filled out insurance forms, the nurse escorted us to a bed surrounded by white curtains. The room smelled antiseptic.

Dr. Monning walked up to me and introduced himself. He asked me several questions and then explained that they would need to take a skull x-ray. A few minutes later, a man in a white uniform gently lifted Darcy onto a small rolling bed and wheeled her into another room.

It seemed like hours later when the technician brought Darcy back. She was still asleep and looked so little in the big bed. Her peaceful face appeared angelic and innocent.

"Oh, Darcy, I hope you're going to be all right." Then I caught myself. *No,* I struggled within myself, *that's not true, is it? I don't want you to be all right. I wonder how sad I'd be if you died. Sometimes I think I hate you. I long to be freed of the responsibilities and burdens of being a mother.* I stopped. *I'm not supposed to feel this way,* I rebuked myself. But I knew I couldn't hold these feelings in any longer. I let my thoughts continue.

I wanted to have a child so much, Darcy. We tried for three years before you were finally conceived, and now I wonder whether I want you around at all. You demand so much from me. Sometimes I just want to be free.

I felt ashamed, but at the same time, it was as if a heavy burden was being lifted from me. I was finally being honest with myself. Tears welled in my eyes.

Darcy, I haven't hurt you for a long time and I'm not going to again...but I still resent you. You seem to want more from me than I'm able to give. I'm trying to trust God for the future but I wonder if I've hurt you permanently, psychologically. I read somewhere that children who have been abused usually grow up to abuse their own children.

Oh, Heavenly Father, I don't want that to happen. Please protect Darcy. Please keep her safe from such a future. You know I never wanted to hurt her. You know I'm sorry. Please forgive me and heal Darcy's inner wounds.

I stared at Darcy. Pulling a handkerchief out of my purse, I wiped my cheeks and blew my nose.

"Kathy, how is she doing?"

Larry's voice startled me. I stood up, turned around, and reached for his hand. "The doctor hasn't said anything yet. Oh, I'm so glad you're here."

A few minutes later, Dr. Monning joined us. "Mr. and Mrs. Miller, Darcy has a concussion, but she's going to be just fine. The skull x-rays show there isn't any damage. You can take her home; just keep an eye on her for the next twenty-four hours. Wake her up through the night every four hours or so, and feel free to call me if you notice anything wrong."

The next day, Darcy played as hard as ever. I watched her and was particularly aware of her bright smile and loving vivaciousness. I began to realize how much I would have missed these moments, and so many others, if anything had happened to her. The realization became stronger as the day progressed and I felt a stirring of love in my heart for her. I knew that I didn't hate her and the sensation of God's forgiveness cleansed my heart.

That night as I tucked her into bed, I stroked her bangs back from her forehead. Love for her overwhelmed me. I wanted to cry with relief.

Darcy, I do love you. I wasn't sure before, but the Lord has shown me how much I really do. It still hurts me to think of how I used to hurt you, but I'm going to trust the Lord to heal my hurt and yours. In the meantime, I know that He has forgiven me.

I kissed her forehead. "Good night, Darcy. Sleep tight." I walked to the door and turned off the light.

"Mommy, I love you," Darcy called.

I turned to face her in the dark. "Oh, Darcy, I love you very much and I'm glad I can say that now and mean it. Good night, honey."

20

Christmas—A Day for Starting Over

December 3

November stepped aside to make room for a festive December. It was hard to believe Christmas would soon be here. Christmas decorations draped the streets and almost every television commercial advertised some new toy or gift. Darcy grew more excited each day thinking that all the toys, dolls, and miscellaneous trinkets were going to be hers.

November had meant celebrating Thanksgiving. But for me every day was a thanksgiving, a time to give thanks and praise to the Lord who was delivering me from my uncontrollable anger.

At the December Christian Women's Club board meeting, Joy announced plans for the board's Christmas party. It was to be a formal evening for couples and sounded exciting. But when she informed us it would be on Tuesday night, December twentieth, I felt disappointment fill my heart. Larry worked on Tuesday nights.

When I mentioned the party to Larry the next day, his saddened face disclosed it would be impossible for him to take the night off. But, somehow, an unexpected peace grew within my heart as I calmly told him, "Sweetheart, I'm sure that if the Lord wants you to go with me, He'll somehow make a way for it to happen."

Larry's skeptical frown almost pricked my ballooning hope, but I reminded myself of Proverbs 3:5-6, which I had been trying to keep at the center of my thoughts for the last week. "Trust in the Lord with all your heart, and do not lean on your own understanding. In all your ways acknowledge Him, and He will make your paths straight." Even if it meant going to the party by myself, I was determined to trust the Lord and not get uptight.

As Christmas drew closer, Mark became increasingly fussy with teething. Just when he had started sleeping consistently through the night, I was once again being awakened by his painful cries.

One Wednesday around midnight, Mark's squall invaded my dream. In a fogged haze of weariness, I pulled myself out of bed and made my way to his room.

Picking him up out of his crib, I soothed, "Oh, Mark, are your teeth hurting again? You are really having a hard time with them, aren't you? Let's go get some aspirin."

After giving him the aspirin, I laid him on my shoulder and sleepily sank down into the rocking chair. As it squeaked softly in the silent, cool night air, I prayed, *Dear Lord, help Mark's gums stop hurting now so that he and I can get back to sleep.*

The placidity enveloped me, and my mind and heart absorbed the loveliness of the moment. Even though my body yearned for the warmth of my bed, my spirit longed to praise the Lord.

Oh, Father, you are doing such marvelous things in my life. I stand in awe at your power...and your forgiveness. Lord, you've forgiven me so many times and yet I know you'll have to forgive me many more times. I smiled. *But at least not as often as before.*

I still experienced eruptions of anger and frustration, but it wasn't unbridled anger anymore. I was gaining control. Life was beautiful and Jesus had never seemed so real to me. My devotions took on a new luster, like the sparkling Christmas ornaments around me. I loved working on the Christian Women's Club board. The Lord used me there and I had a purpose for living. Even though my marriage wasn't exactly the way I wanted it to be, I believed the Lord was going to make it a lot better one day. I just had to wait for His timing. For right now, I was content to continue accepting Larry as he was and to work on attaining greater patience and joy.

I was loved and that love was flowing onto Darcy. I still battled anger, frustration, and stress, but instead of believing that I was losing the battle, I knew I had won the war. Victory was mine to claim. Life was challenging and exciting.

The impact of my reverie cascaded into my soul like a waterfall streaming down rocks into a clear, sparkling pool. My heart burst with thanksgiving and joy. "Lord, you are delivering me. I am not abusing my child any longer. I am being set free," I whispered.

Tears trickled down my cheeks and I hugged Mark tighter. I kissed his head. *Thank you, Jesus. Thank you. I'm so grateful. I love you so much. Thank you for loving me during this past year even when I didn't deserve it. The joy I'm experiencing in this moment is worth the wait of all those months.*

Without realizing it, a song began to form on my lips. "Turn your eyes upon Jesus, look full in his wonderful face. And the things of earth will grow strangely dim in the light of his glory and grace."

Oh, Jesus, yes, your glory and grace wipe out all the pain and sorrow of this year. You've touched me. I love you.

Many songs filled my mind as my joy sought expression. Mark was asleep but I wasn't concerned that I might wake him. I wanted to wake the whole world. I wanted everyone to know: *Jesus is in control of my life!*

The next couple of days were filled with shopping, baking, and sending out Christmas cards. Christmas was approaching all too fast; and dinner at my home for ten family members was foremost in my thoughts and plans. I hadn't had time to even think about the board's Christmas party.

Then, unexpectedly, one day, Larry said, "You'll never guess what my boss told me last night. I have too many vacation hours on the books and have to take some time off before the new year. Isn't that wild?"

I jerked my head toward him. "Honey," I exclaimed, "that's the answer to my prayer. Now you can go to the board Christmas party. Can you ask for next Tuesday, the twentieth, off?"

He smiled. "Yeah, that's right. That's great! Sure I can."

I could barely sit still as I grinned at him. *Thank you, Jesus; you did it. I trusted you and you did it.*

Larry's smile grew as I hugged him. "Kathy," he replied, "the Lord has rewarded your faith. I wasn't sure that He could do it but He did."

My excitement grew all that week after Larry confirmed he could have the night off.

On Tuesday evening we arrived at the fancy restaurant of a local hotel. I was truly grateful that Larry was beside me as we ate the delicious food and enjoyed the special entertainment.

Five days later, on Christmas morning, Darcy woke us early. She was so excited about seeing what Santa Claus had brought her. Instructing her to stay in her room, Larry, my mother, and I turned on the Christmas tree lights and made sure the camera was ready to capture her delight as she reacted to her presents. I opened the drapes. The dawn's soft, pink light filtered into the room, creating a fairyland effect on the presents and the tree. The blinking lights of the tree cast red, blue, and orange shadows on the walls, and my spirit was illuminated with hope and joy.

Christmas morning... the day we celebrate our Savior's birth and the first step in His journey for our salvation. And this was the morning of the birth of a life free from hurting

Darcy, free from uncontrolled anger, free from condemnation and hate.

As a cocoon opens to reveal a ready-to-fly butterfly, my life was opening also—opening to love, self-esteem, faith, and patience.

Christmas morning, the beginning of salvation for mankind—and the beginning of an abundant new life for me.

Epilogue

Two months later, from February tenth through the twelfth, God performed the miracle that I had been trusting him for—the healing of my marriage.

On that particular weekend, Larry and I attended a marriage-encounter seminar that revitalized our relationship and reassured me that Larry did truly love me after all. I learned that all my doubts and fears about his love were unfounded. And we were reunited in a oneness that we hadn't experienced since the early days of our marriage. What had been a fragile thread of communication between us became a steel cable as we learned over the following months how to share our feelings with each other. It was a process of growth—painful at times—but worth the effort.

As a bonus, my self-esteem was raised even higher as I experienced God's love and forgiveness in an even greater way than I had before. After that precious weekend, Larry and I became involved in the seminar's volunteer organization, and two years later, the Lord directed us to become involved in Christian Marriage Communication which presents a similar kind of weekend seminar. Our unity grew as we served the Lord in that ministry.

In the ensuing years, I've seen God continue to teach me more about dealing with anger, frustration, and stress. This, too, was a continuing process of growth that seemed to move slowly at times. Being the kind of mother I want to be is still a difficult, conscious choice of demonstrating unconditional love and spending quality time with Darcy and Mark. But, little by little, that choice becomes easier.

I'm trusting the Lord and seeing His miracles work in my relationship with Darcy. The Lord is healing our relationship and now we're good friends in addition to being mother and daughter. One of my strongest desires is to accept her always as she is—independent and strong-willed—because, in the past, I wasn't able to do that. Now, through God's grace, I'm learning.

Being a parent is definitely one of the most difficult jobs on earth. And of all jobs, it has the most at stake—the lives of unique individuals. Happy is the parent who believes God's promise that "children are a gift of the Lord; the fruit of the womb is a reward" (Psalm 127:3). Patience and understanding may require focusing on the pleasant times that we have experienced with our children, and we can comfort ourselves with the knowledge that we are sharing in the tremendous joy of seeing a human being mature before our eyes.

As I see my children grow, I am learning to give myself credit for the times when I am a good mother and to forgive myself when I fail. I'm also growing in my ability to live in the power of the Holy Spirit, moment by moment.

When my anger was out of control, I thought that what I experienced could never be used for good or for God's glory. But God is a creative God and can work all things for good. Now I experience a deep satisfaction and an inexpressible joy as I see God work through me to minister to others.

To God belongs all praise and glory.

If you would like to write to me, please do so. I'd love to hear from you.

Kathy Collard Miller
P.O. Box 1058
Placentia, CA 92670

Appendix I

- **How to Deal with Anger**
- **When Stress Becomes Distress**
- **How to Cope with Worry**

There's no denying, child abuse is prevalent in our society. Among the causes, the following have been listed by those who have studied this issue in great detail:
- Parent has been abused as a child (although this is not true in all cases; it was not true in my own case);
- Parent is socially isolated and rarely has time away from the children;
- Parent has experienced a series of changes or crises and, as a result, feels depressed, lonely, and/or fearful;
- Parent demonstrates an inability to cope with stress;
- Parent receives little support from other family members;
- Parent has troubled relationship with spouse;
- Parent lacks knowledge about child development and effective discipline;
- Parent holds a negative attitude toward the child;
- Parent suffers from low self-esteem;
- Parent has perfectionist tendencies which lead to unrealistic expectations for self and child.

Researchers have also found that a child's crying is the behavior that most upsets abusive parents; problems associated with toilet training are second. When a parent cannot successfully quiet or potty train a child, anxiety and frustration build up in the parent, and anger often surfaces.

How to Deal with Anger

Psychologist H. Norman Wright defines anger as a strong emotion of displeasure that often results from frustration or from having a goal blocked. People frequently equate anger with losing control, and many Christians call that sin.

I agree that if we lose control, the uncontrolled behavior is sin and should be confessed. But on my road to victory over anger, I discovered that learning to distinguish between the attitude of anger and the feeling of anger gave me more control over my actions.

If we call all anger wrong then we are apt to repress all angry feelings lest we sin. But doing that will only make us more angry, because anger that is buried alive usually resurfaces later.

Instead, we can recognize that the first flash of anger within us is a feeling (not an attitude) of anger that is neither right nor wrong. We have little control over a feeling that flares up within us. This is different, however, from an attitude of anger, which results from a decision not to deal with the feeling. Not recognizing, confronting, or dealing with an angry feeling can prevent understanding of it, which, in turn, can lead to long-term resentment, bitterness, or rage.

Ephesians 4:26-27 states, "If you are angry, don't sin by nursing your grudge. Don't let the sun go down with you still angry—get over it quickly; for when you are angry you give a mighty foothold to the devil."

I believe this verse emphasizes my point. It implies that we are going to get angry, and anger isn't wrong as long as we deal with it. It's what we do with our feeling of anger that determines whether or not we will sin.

Once we feel the first flash of anger, we can react in three ways. We can *deny*, *direct*, or *declare* the emotion.

Denying the anger is a destructive way of dealing with it. This action only causes the anger to be repressed. Ignoring anger does not make it go away.

A second way of dealing with anger, directing it, can be either healthy or destructive. If we use the energy that is stimulated by anger to accomplish tasks like cleaning the house or pulling weeds but fail to examine the cause of our anger and take action to control the emotion, then we are directing our anger in an unhealthy, destructive way. However, if we first direct the anger but cope with it after the initial surge of energy has subsided, then we are reacting in a healthy, positive manner.

Declaring anger in a constructive way is by far the best way to deal with anger. We want to accept responsibility for our anger and react in such a way that we demonstrate full awareness and control of our emotions. It is important to communicate our angry feelings with an honest, yet loving approach.

Let me share a four-step process that can help you react to anger in healthy ways.

The first step is to *realize angry feelings*. In other words, be aware of red flag warnings, those feelings we have before we reach the point of losing control and blowing our cool.

For instance, fifteen minutes before I explode, I find that I'm usually worried about a time schedule or some other pressure in my life. At ten minutes before, I feel tense and hurried, and my chest muscles feel tight. When I'm gritting my teeth and raising my voice in quick, terse commands, I know my five-minute warning is signaling.

If we can get in the habit of acknowledging our own unique red-flag warnings, we'll be able to recognize when our fifteen-minute countdown has begun and we can proceed to the second step.

The second step is to *magnetize our mind away from our anger*, and the physical tension and increased energy it often causes, with a *distraction*. A distraction, any activity that helps us turn our attention away from our anger, is used to allow a brief cooling down period and relieve the anger before it is negatively directed toward another person.

Here are a few possible distractions:

- take a vigorous walk
- run in place
- hit a pillow or a punching bag
- take a shower—with or without screaming
- sing loudly
- take ten slow, deep breaths and count them out loud
- play a musical instrument
- recite an uplifting Bible verse
- telephone a friend, a hot line, or a professional counselor.

The third step is to *recognize the underlying cause of our anger.* In many cases, when the situation is examined closely, we find that the immediate circumstances are not the real cause of our anger. Instead, we realize that we have focused our anger away from the real cause and toward a readily available, but perhaps inappropriate, target.

When trying to determine the actual cause of my anger, I find it helpful to have a mental checklist of possible causes. For example:

- *Physical.* Am I tired? Do I need some exercise?
- *Psychological.* Am I thinking negatively about something? Am I worried? Is some relationship troubling me? Are my expectations for myself unrealistic?
- *Spiritual.* Am I not trusting God? Do I have some unconfessed sin?

Once the actual cause has been determined, we can move on to the fourth step which is to *verbalize our anger in an appropriate way.*

We can do this by using "I" messages instead of "you" messages. "I" messages express feelings and opinions— they reveal needs—without expecting the other person to change and without telling the other person what to do (unless that person asks how he or she can help). "You" messages like, "You make me angry," or "You shouldn't do that," accuse and often provoke a negative reaction. Although it is difficult not to blame or have expectations of the person to whom our anger is directed, we can find strength by trusting God for the circumstances of our lives.

Another way to safely and constructively express our anger is to write down our negative thoughts and feelings. Often this will be enough to release the anger. But if not, it can be a good way to prepare for sharing our anger in a calm way.

Going through this four-step process each time we feel ourselves becoming angry will help to ensure that we will be in control of our anger instead of allowing our anger to be in control of us.

When Stress Becomes Distress

When trying to understand and control anger in our lives, we must consider stress. Each one of us is under a tremendous amount of stress, and stress in itself is not wrong. It is when we allow stress to overpower us in such a way that we react negatively—when stress becomes distress— that we are in danger of becoming out of control.

What Is Stress?

Stress can be defined as any condition or situation that imposes demands for change upon us. Did you know that we are even under stress when we are sleeping? No one is ever without stress. It is a part of every aspect of our lives. We can even look upon stress as positive because it can strengthen our relationship with God as we turn to Him for help. However, it is important to recognize when stress becomes distress in our lives, because it's likely we are not trusting God in that situation.

What Causes Stress?

First, there are expectations—what we expect from ourselves, what we think others expect of us, and what we think God expects of us.

Without realizing it, my melancholy temperament had led me to expect perfection from myself all my life. And each time I didn't meet that unrealistic standard, my self-esteem took a beating.

When I became a Christian, this problem increased. After all, didn't I have the power of God to make me holy and perfect? Didn't God command me to be holy as He is holy?

And when I became a mother, I thought I should always be happy with my baby and never be upset with her. I feared that any sign of my displeasure would destroy her self-image.

These issues tore down my self-esteem as I saw how imperfect I was. Now, I am able to realize that no one is perfect; we are all in the process of growth. And I accept that although I will never reach perfection here on earth, I am learning to become more like Christ in my daily walk of faith.

What others expect of us can be stressful, too. When I couldn't control my anger toward Darcy, I didn't want to tell anyone because I didn't want my image as a mature Christian woman to be destroyed. In addition, I thought confessing my sin would somehow stain God's reputation. After all, if I was having trouble, didn't that mean God wasn't powerful enough to help me, or others?

Now I know that I shouldn't live my life by what others think of me or expect from me. I should live my life under God's rule. Understanding this has freed me to let others know when I'm hurting so they can pray for me and help me. I realize that usually others don't judge me as harshly as I judge myself. And we can benefit from the help of those who care.

But what about God and His expectations of us? Even

though He has called us to be holy as He is holy, He also realizes we are in a process of growth. Only Jesus is perfect. No one else has been or ever will be. God is not surprised or shocked when it takes us a while to gain victory in a problem area of our lives. It is important for us to understand that He doesn't get upset or condemn us when we sin. If we think He does, we will try to rationalize, excuse, or justify our sin in some way. Instead, God wants us to ask forgiveness and go on living in the power of the Holy Spirit.

How to Cope with Worry

Another stressful factor in our lives is worry. When we worry, our thoughts are most often concerned with the past or the future, not the present. So we worry in vain because worrying can't help the future or change the past.

But how do we deal with worry. First, when we start to worry, we can think of the worst possible thing that could happen. Then we can think of reasons why the situation we're worried about wouldn't be so terrible after all. You see, worry is rooted in the vagueness of a situation. But if we go ahead and think of the situation's conclusion, often what we feared doesn't seem so bad after all.

Second, we can claim Romans 8:28: "And we know that God causes all things to work together for good to those who love God, to those who are called according to his purpose."

We can let go of our worry because God is in control of our lives if we allow Him to be. If He lets what we fear happen, it means He has a better plan. Remembering how much He loves us will help us realize He'll use that plan for our good.

The third strategy for coping with worry is not to take on a responsibility that God doesn't intend for us to have. I have discovered that when I'm worried about something I think my husband should be doing, I am trying to assume the responsibility for him. But doing that causes anxiety and fear in me and doesn't allow God to work in my husband's life, because I'm in the way—and I'm usually nagging.

The last cause of stress I'll mention is allowing ourselves to become too busy. This is a real temptation for Christians because we see how valuable and necessary so many Christian projects are. And people like me, who have a hard time saying no, think that if they don't do it personally, the job won't get done. Remember, "A need is not necessarily a call."

It is also important as we deal with stress to make sure we are filled and empowered by the Holy Spirit. Although Christians are indwelt by the Holy Spirit from the moment of their salvation, they may not necessarily be controlled by Him unless they submit their lives to Him. We can do that simply by asking Him to fill us and by making moment by moment decisions to let Him control our lives.

Reach Out for Help

Anger, stress, and abusive actions don't have to be a part of our lives. I encourage you to reach out for the help you need if anger is a problem for you. Seek someone with whom you feel comfortable sharing your problem, preferably a professional Christian counselor. And keep in mind that God is always there with you. He wants to offer you the help and hope that you need. He came to my rescue. I know that He can help you, too.

Appendix II

Helpful Resources for Moms

CHILDHELP USA
6463 Independence Avenue
Woodland Hills, CA 91367
(818) 347-7280

Meets the physical, emotional, educational, and spiritual needs of abused and neglected children and their families through several programs including the CHILDHELP Family Evaluation Program.

Depression After Delivery
Box 1282
Morrisville, PA 19067
(215) 295-3994; after 9 p.m. hot line: **(609) 585-2244**

Offers help for mothers experiencing post-partum depression and educates the public about the problem.
Publication: Depression after Delivery (quarterly newsletter).
Services: Annual conference; local support groups.

Family Resource Coalition
230 N. Michigan Ave., Suite 1625,
Chicago, IL 60601
(312) 726-4750

Serves as a clearing house for about 500 parent education and support programs, including grass roots organizations and those affiliated with universities and hospitals.
Publications: FRC Report (three issues a year), Connections (bimonthly update).
Services: Biannual conference.

La Leche League International, Inc.
9616 Minneapolis Ave.,
Franklin Park, IL 60131
24-hour hot line: **(312) 455-7730**

Specializes in encouraging breastfeeding mothers, as well as mothers who wish to "put family first."
Publication: New Beginnings magazine.
Services: Publications; conferences; local support groups.

MOPS Outreach, Inc.
4175 Harlan St., Suite 105
Wheatridge, CO 80033-5150;
(303) 420-6100 (information)

Offers charter to local churches for groups that help mothers of preschoolers find friendship, express creativity and grow as a person.
Publication: The Love Knot newsletter.
Services: Biannual convention; leadership training seminars; handbooks; preschool program (MOPPETS); local support groups.

Mothers At Home
Box 2208
Merrifield, VA 22116
(703) 352-2292

Helps equip mothers who choose to stay home with children and educates the public about mothering.
Publications: Welcome Home.
Services: Publications, research projects, speakers' bureau, local support groups.

Mothers of Twins
12404 Princess Jeanne, NE
Albuquerque, NM 87112
(505) 275-0955

Provides information and support in parenting of twins.
Publication: MOTC S Notebook (quarterly).
Services: Local newsletters; literature library; annual convention; clothing and equipment exchanges; annual philanthropic project; local support groups.

Mothers Center Development Project
129 Jackson Street
Hempstead, NY 14550
(800) 645-3828; (516) 486-6614

Serves as a hot line for mothers who wish to start groups in which information and ideas are shared, bolstered by the expertise of child-care professionals.
Publication: The Mothers Center Inter-Center Newsletter Journal (local groups produce own newsletters).
Services: Annual conference.

National Child Abuse Hot line
1-800-4-A-CHILD

A counselling and referral service staffed by professional crisis counselors and also functions as a nationally recognized "triage" point, receiving calls and referring them to other organizations in the field of abuse and neglect.

Parents' Anonymous of California
7120 Franklin Avenue
Los Angeles, CA 90046
Hot line: (800) 352-0386

An international organization for the prevention and treatment of child abuse and neglect. Provides self-help groups designed to give parents the support they need to prevent them from hurting their children.

Parents Without Partners
7910 Woodman Ave., Suite 1000
Bethesda, MD 20814
(800) 638-8078 (information)

Studies the problems and solutions of single parenting.

The Salvation Army
Attn: A/Captain Margaret E. Doughty
120 West 14th St.
New York, NY 10011
(212) 337-7383

Publications: Catalog of Resources for Strengthening the Family; A Child in Our Midst—A Study Course On Keeping Children Safe From Abuse.

For additional information regarding child development and child abuse write:

American Humane Association
Children's Division
5351 South Roslyn St.
Englewood, CO 80201

Association for Childhood Education International
3615 Wisconsin Ave., NW
Washington, DC 20016

Bank Street College of Education
610 West 112th St.
New York, NY 10025

Child Welfare League of America
67 Irving Place
New York, NY 10003

**Day Care & Child Development Council
of America, Inc.**
1401 K Street, NW
Washington, DC 20005

**Merrill-Palmer Institute of
Human Development and Family Life**
71 East Ferry Ave.
Detroit, MI 48202

**National Association for the
Education of Young Children**
1834 Connecticut Ave. NW
Washington, DC 20009

National Committee for the
Prevention of Child Abuse
Box 2866
Chicago, IL 60690

New York City Agency for Child Development
Human Resources Administration
240 Church St., Room 313
New York, NY 10013

Office of Child Development, HEW
National Center for Child Advocacy
Administration for Children, Youth and Families
Box 1182
Washington, DC 20013

Questions for Individual or Group Study

The following questions have been designed to give additional insight into the frustrations of parenting and how anger that rages out of control could lead to abusive behavior. Please use a notebook to record your comments. Discussion of these questions is not intended to take the place of seeking additional help from friends, pastors, and professional counsel if the problem of child abuse occurs in your home.

Chapter 1—I Just Want to Be a Good Mom

1. Little Darcy didn't like getting her hair washed and Mom was exhausted from the pressures of the day, two signs that point to potential trouble. Is bath time and hair-washing an unpleasant experience for you and your youngsters? What other areas of daily routine are unpleasant? What are some steps you could take to alleviate some of the pressures and unpleasantness of daily routine?

2. Mom's outlet for her tension and exhaustion was spanking her child, which, at times, became uncontrolled beating. What kinds of positive ways can you find for expending the tensions and exhaustion that may engulf you from time to time?

3. Part of Mom's stress lay in the fact that being Christian and leading Bible studies did not make her immune to becoming angry and out of control. "People think I'm a strong Christian; how can I be acting like this?" she stated.

Do you ever find yourself feeling just like this mom? She was not perfect and neither are you. Even the Apostle Paul experienced feelings of imperfection. "I don't understand myself at all, for I really want to do what is right, but I can't. I do what I don't want to—what I hate" (Romans 7:15-16, *TLB*).

Realizing we're not perfect does not excuse us from mistreating our children, or anyone else for that matter. It may help us to understand, however, that it's possible, from time to time, to act in a manner unbecoming to our heavenly Father and that we must come to Him again and again for forgiveness. "So overflowing is his kindness towards us that he took away all our sins through the blood of his Son, by whom we are saved; and he has showered down upon us the richness of his grace" (Ephesians 1:7-8, *TLB*).

Chapter 2—But You Promised You'd Babysit the Kids!

1. Time out from daily routine is important for everyone. List some of the ways you enjoy taking time out.

2. Sometimes it's not always easy to find someone to keep your children. List some of the people who are available for you to call on. Are there friends with whom you could trade babysitting? Are there places you could go for rest and relaxation that offer child care?

3. Handling disappointment is something we all have to do at one time or another. How do you most often handle disappointments? Are you able to accept when things don't go the way you'd like them to? What are some of the steps you could take to handle disappointments in a more positive way?

4. Mom felt that she wasn't first in her husband's life. Do you think this added to her frustrations? Are you number one in your husband's life? Or do you feel second to the children, his job, his friends and activities? What are some of the things you can do to place yourself higher on his list of priorities? What place does your husband have in your life? Is he number one? Or does he fall somewhere between the children and your activities? What are some of the things you can do to show your husband he's number one with you?

5. Later in this chapter, we see Mom trying to reach out to a friend for support. Instead of receiving encouragement to talk further, Mom was forced to experience more guilt and retreated within herself. Have you ever found yourself in a similar experience? If so, are you reluctant to reach out again?

6. Sometimes it's hard to recognize a person's plea for help. Sometimes we recognize the plea but don't know how to respond. What are some ways we can be available to love and encourage others when they're reaching out for help?

Chapter 3—Whatever Happened to the Joys of Motherhood?

1. What kinds of expectations have you placed on the role of motherhood? Is it all you thought it would be? List some of the positive experiences you've had since becoming a mother. Now list some of your disappointments.

2. What kinds of formal training did you receive to become a mother? If you're like the rest of us you didn't receive much training, if any. Therefore, for many of us it's by trial and error. And because of that, we're going to do some things right and some things wrong. In this chapter, Mom

struggled with potty training her daughter. Now, potty-training in itself can cause frustrations for any mother, but in this case, our mother was already upset by other things surrounding her. From what you've read already, can you list some of those frustrations?

3. Is it possible our mother was not so much battling with her daughter's failure to use the potty chair as she was peer pressure, a bent toward perfectionism, a feeling that she wasn't number one in her husband's life? Are any of those frustrations evident in your own life? What were some of the reasons Mom gave for not going to someone for help?

4. It appears that Mommy's little girl was not ready to be potty-trained. Perhaps there were other areas in her life, because of her young age and unique personality, she was being pushed into. In looking at your own children, are there areas where you expect more from them than their age is able to handle? In what areas would it be possible to ease up on your expectations and give them more time to develop and mature?

Chapter 4—Where Did My Clean House Go?

1. Have you ever asked the question, Why did I have kids anyway? Perhaps you've felt like you'll never have a clean house again. Or that your children tie you down and stand in the way of your having a good time. Can you think of times when you've had plans made only to have to change them because of an unexpected illness in your child? How did you handle your disappointment? If you reacted negatively how could you have handled the situation differently?

2. Mom was reminded about the importance of memorizing God's Word. Do you have favorite passages from Scripture that help you in times of disappointment?

Chapter 5—Lord, Help My Unbelief

1. Have you ever bargained with God? How did the circumstance turn out?

2. Remembering she had hurt her daughter earlier in this chapter, Mom apologizes for getting angry with her. Do you think she was truly sorry for her actions? What would indicate that she was—or wasn't?

How important is it to be able to say I'm sorry to your children? Do you find it difficult or easy to apologize to your children? Have you ever done any of the following while you've apologized to your child?

- Incorporate your child's name into your apology.

- Look the child directly in the eye.

- Hold your child close as you apologize.

- Follow your apology with a hug.

3. Mom admitted that "worrying didn't do a bit of good." Does worry play an important part in your life? Can you think of times when you worried to no avail? How could you have handled the situation differently? Are you familiar with the Scripture that says: "Casting all your anxieties upon Him, because He cares for you" (2 Peter 5:7)? Is there a situation in your life right now that you need to turn over to Him completely, casting all your cares upon Him?

Chapter 6—A Soap Opera and A Bag of M & M's®

1. In this chapter, we find several elements adding to Mom's frustrations. List some of those elements. Was our Mom

responsible for all the elements that caused her frustration? Are any of these same elements present in your life?

2. What did our young Mom do to escape from the frustrations and daily routine in her life? In her case, how was this beneficial or detrimental to her well-being?

3. How do you escape from some of the frustrations and daily routine in your own life? How are they beneficial or detrimental to your well-being and the well-being of your family?

4. Be creative and list other positive "ways of escape."

Chapter 7—A Glimmer of Hope

1. In the beginning of this chapter, we read, "A warning bell in my brain signaled potential danger." What do you suppose our author meant by this statement? Have you had similar experiences? If so, how did you respond to the "warning bell"?

2. Our young mom found that much of her irritability and fatigue as of late was due to the sugar she was consuming and in the fact that she was not eating nutritious meals. If you find yourself tired and irritable much of the time, could the reason be poor nutrition?

3. What changes could you make in your daily routine to ensure that you and your family are eating nutritious foods and getting the proper amount of rest?

4. Our young mom vowed to give up those things in her life that took away from her well-being and her time with her family? Is God asking you to make some sacrifices in your life right now that would make a difference for the better in your home?

Chapter 8—Punishment Is Retribution, But Discipline Is Training

1. How important is it to live up to our promises to our children? In this chapter, Mom promised to play a game with her daughter. Could her other duties have waited until after she played with her daughter? In this case, Mom had a schedule to meet. How could she have arranged to meet this schedule in other ways?

2. There are some activities, like the game Candyland, that seem never to end. For fun, can you name others? Now, list activities that are short and enjoyable for you and your child to do together.

3. What seem to be contributing factors to little Darcy's behavior in this chapter? Our Mom felt entirely responsible for her little girl's actions. Do you feel she is right or wrong? Explain your answer.

4. Why did cleaning the house seem more important to Mom than paying attention to her daughter? Can you relate to her feelings?

5. How is punishment defined in this chapter? How is discipline defined? How did the difference between the two help our mom in how she reacted to her daughter's behavior?

Chapter 9—At Times It's Difficult, But I'm Learning to Say No

1. Saying no was difficult for this Mom and it's probably difficult for many of you. What reasons did our mom state for having a hard time saying no to teaching Sunday School? Do you find yourself accepting more commitments than you can handle? What steps could you take to elimi-

nate some of the commitments you've already made? What can you do to ensure not taking on too many commitments in the future?

2. Here are some suggestions for learning to say no:

● Practice saying the word *no* over and over; the more you say it, the easier it will roll off your tongue when the need arises.

● Don't feel compelled to give someone your answer immediately upon request. Take some time to think it over and see if what you're being asked to do will fit into your already busy schedule.

● Make a list of priorities in your life. Then ask yourself if what you're being asked to do will serve to enhance what you've chosen as being important to you and your family.

● Learn to detect "warning bells" when being asked to do something. If you're not feeling right about it from the beginning, it's probably a good indicator that you need to say no.

● Memorize the statement: *A need is not necessarily a call.*

Can you list other tips in learning to say no?

Chapter 10—Lord, Why Won't You Change My Husband?

1. What were the causes of Mom's disappointment and frustration in this chapter? Were her frustrations justified? How did she react to her disappointment and anger? Were her actions justified?

2. Have you ever asked God to change someone in your life?

What were the results of your request? How have you dealt with how God answered your prayer?

Chapter 11—What a Relief to Have Others Know

1. Have you ever felt extreme anger toward one of your children? Do you think this is unique to yourself? How do you know if it is or isn't?

2. This chapter listed some constructive ways to deal with anger. What are they? Can you think of others?

3. Have you ever discussed your feelings of anger with anyone? Make a list of those with whom you've spoken in the past. What kinds of responses did you receive?

4. Our author's friend Sally was perceptive to her need to talk. Do you have a friend like Sally? Is there someone who you feel could use a listening ear and positive encouragement? How could you make yourself available to that person?

5. In this chapter, our young mom was encouraged to use "I messages" in communicating with her family members. What are "I messages"? What are "you messages"? What kinds of messages do you most often use in your daily encounters?

Chapter 12—I'll Show Them My Love

1. In this chapter, how did our mom react to the heat of the day and the tension she was feeling? List some of the positive ways you can choose to react to stress in your life?

2. Mom expressed that she didn't feel loved. What were her reasons for feeling unloved? She said to God in prayer, "I know about your unconditional love, but I don't feel it." What do you know about God's unconditional love? Are you

having a hard time feeling His love because of circumstances in your life?

3. Mom decided to have a surprise birthday party for her
husband. What are some other ways we can show love to
our family members? (Keep in mind that some ways to
show our love take much time and planning and are done
on an occasional basis; others take little effort at all on our
part and can be done on a daily basis.)

Chapter 13—The Party Was a Success, But the Price Was High

1. Do you think the birthday party for Dad was a success?
Explain your answer.

2. Looking back over this chapter, are there things Mom
could have done differently that might have eased some of
the tension she was feeling?

3. What was Dad's reaction to the surprise party? Do you
think it was the response our young mom was looking for?

Chapter 14—Love Is a Choice, Not a Feeling

1. What was our young dad's reason for not going to the
neighborhood barbecue and not being able to spend more
time with his family? Is this situation typical for a young
family?

2. Mom decided to go to the neighborhood picnic even
though Dad couldn't go. Do you think this was a good
idea? Explain your answer.

3. Mom asked the question: Can love exist alongside hate?
How would you answer that?

4. Would it be helpful for you to make a list of those things

children the ages of yours can be expected to do and post it where you can be reminded daily? Considering the age(s) of your child(ren), what would you put on your list?

Chapter 15—It's a Growth Process—For My Child *and* Me

1. There are many resources that show evidence that men and women think and react differently from one another. Dr. Tim LaHaye's book *Understanding the Male Temperament* was the resource that pointed these differences out to our young mom. Have you come across any of these resources? If so, how have you found them helpful?

2. Make a list of the seven steps Mom used to help her get a handle on the areas of anger, bitterness, and resentment in her life. How can you use this list of seven steps to help in your own circumstances? Which of the seven steps do you find most difficult to follow? Which for you is easiest to follow?

3. Have you ever considered making a "blessings" list? Would you like to do so now?

4. Mom found that tacking up reminders throughout the house helped her to control her angry feelings. What specific reminders did she post? Is this something you could do to help in your own home? Perhaps even in your car?

5. Growth is a process. Are you willing to give yourself and your family members the necessary time it takes in this growth process?

Chapter 16—Success Happens One Day at a Time

1. List the causes of greatest frustration at the beginning of this chapter for our young mom. How did she handle these frustrations?

2. In her growth process, Mom had set-backs. Did she give up? What did she do?

3. How did Mom encourage herself? What indicated she was on her way to victory?

Chapter 17—God Loves Me and So Do I!

1. What were the indications in this chapter that the Lord was leading our young mom in a new direction? How did she respond to the various signs?

2. At last, she came to the realization of God's love for her. How did she express this realization?

3. What had caused Mom to think God had stopped loving her? For some reason, are you struggling with the thought that God may not love you? Our young mom said to the Lord, "I'm important to you and you accept me as I am." Will you make that claim for yourself right now?

Chapter 18—On My Way to Victory

1. There are pros and cons to the issue of spanking. Some parents choose to spank, others choose to discipline by taking away privileges, grounding, etc. Our young mom chose to spank her child for misbehavior in certain cases. How was her method of spanking in this chapter different from earlier chapters?

2. After the spanking, what were the reactions of both mother and child? How were these reactions different from earlier chapters?

3. Mom was finding over and over that God's immediate peace was always available to her as soon as she relaxed in His control. What did that mean for the mom in our story? What does that mean for you?

4. "Everything wasn't perfect like I had intended, but she [Darcy] didn't notice and neither did anyone else," said Mom regarding her little girl's birthday party. Do you think Mom was learning not to place so much emphasis on having her house spotless and everything done just right? How do you know? Is this an area in which you need to relax? How do you know?

Chapter 19—A New Love for My Child

1. Some difficult but honest thoughts were expressed by our young mom in this chapter. What were some of the struggles she was feeling? Have similar thoughts ever gone through your mind?

2. "I'm going to trust the Lord to heal my hurt and yours," expressed Mom to her little girl. If there are hurts in your life and in those of your children, can you trust the Lord to heal them? He's there for you, just like He was and continues to be for the young mom in our story. He's leading her to victory and He wants to do the same for you!

Chapter 20—Christmas—A Day for Starting Over

1. Mom expressed that she still experienced anger and frustrations, but what indicated that she was "being set free"?

2. Christmas . . . the day we celebrate the birth of Christ and the first step in His journey for our salvation. Do you have the joy of knowing this Christ who was born so that we might live and who died so that we might have life eternal with our heavenly Father? If you do, then His power to heal you and set you on the path to victory is yours for the asking. Trust Him with your life and know that His timing is always best. If you don't know Christ, then we invite you to express this prayer: *Jesus, I want to know you and the*

power of your healing love. Please come into my life, remove my guilt and shame, and set me on the pathway to victory. In Jesus' name. Amen.

A Note From the Publisher

Dear Reader: It is our prayer that you have come to a better understanding of how child abuse can happen due to the frustrations of daily pressures and the inability to deal properly with anger, stress, and worry. There is help, just as Kathy Collard Miller and her family have experienced. That help is available to you, too. May the reading of this book be the first step in God's placing you on your pathway to victory!